Stress and achieve more

harriet griffey

the art of
concentration

This edition first published 2010 by Rodale
an imprint of Pan Macmillan, a division of Macmillan Publishers Limited
Pan Macmillan, 20 New Wharf Road, London N1 9RR
Basingstoke and Oxford
Associated companies throughout the world
www.panmacmillan.com

ISBN 978-1-9057-4443-5

1 3 5 7 9 8 6 4 2

A CIP catalogue record for this book is available from the British Library.

Printed and bound in Great Britain by CPI Mackays, Chatham ME5 8TD

This book is intended as a reference volume only, not as a medical manual.
The information given here is designed to help you make informed decisions
about your health. It is not intended as a substitute for any treatment that you
may have been prescribed by your doctor. If you suspect you have a medical
problem, we urge you to seek competent medical help.

Mention of specific companies, organizations or authorities in this book does
not imply endorsement of the publisher, nor does mention of specific companies,
organizations or authorities in the book imply that they endorse the book.

Addresses, websites and telephone numbers given in this book
were correct at the time of going to press.

Visit **www.panmacmillan.com** to read more about all our books and to
buy them. You will also find features, author interviews and news of any
author events, and you can sign up for e-newsletters so that you're
always first to hear about our new releases.

LIVE YOUR WHOLE LIFE™

We inspire and enable people to improve their lives and the world around them

For D.K.B. – he knows why.

Acknowledgements

This book started as a conversation between myself and Liz Gough, Editorial Director at Rodale, and continued with a year of exploration and discovery as I researched and pondered (and eventually wrote) on whether the art of concentration is possible to learn, and how to do it – stretching my own ability along the way! It is a subject that has engaged scientists, philosophers, psychologists, social commentators, teachers, coaches and parents alike, paving the way for a book that aims to provide both context and content to foster the art of concentration, and practical, accessible ways to go about it. Particular acknowledgement is due to some of the ideas and work of various people cited and referenced in the book who contributed to this continuing conversation, including, but in no particular order, the Dalai Llama, Dr Alex Richardson, Carl Honoré, Dr Liz Miller, Professor Jim Horne, Professor Mihaly Csikszentmihalyi, Ian Morris, Linda Stone, David Lynch, Professor Stephen Kaplan, Dr Dharma Singh Khalsa, Professor Norman Ruby, Professor Uta Frith, Sarah-Jayne Blakemore, Dr David Servan-Schreiber, Linda Stone, Professor Fred Gage, Dr William Stixrud and Steve Biddulph.

I also want to acknowledge the work of an exceptional charity, Youth at Risk, and in particular Tony Weekes, Ellie Garraway and Sue Handley, who trained me as a coach and allowed me the privilege of working with them and the students of the schools where I have worked on their behalf. It has been a huge but very enjoyable learning curve that has, in its own small way, contributed to the writing of this book.

Others have contributed in less formal ways, through conversations, ideas and insights, and I would like to thank Susan Clark Every, Tony Visconti (for introducing me to the Alexander Technique), Sue Machell, Beatrice Hollyer, Nina Grunfeld, Simon Lubin, Steven Shaw (for teaching me to swim properly), Anna Johnson, Karen Liebreich and Clare Whittaker (for being the world's best Pilates teacher and physio, and rescuing my back). Thanks are also due to David Buckley for his occasional, much needed and very welcome distraction.

Lastly, my own children, Josh and Robbie, are a constant reminder that whatever we face every day, whether excitement, challenge or change, what lies at the heart of what matters most are those we love.

Contents

INTRODUCTION
Why concentration matters

Give me six hours to chop down a tree and I will
spend the first four sharpening the axe.
Abraham Lincoln

There is more to life than increasing its speed.
Mahatma Gandhi

Shaped by nature and nurture, your ability to concentrate – or not – will have a dramatic impact on the way you view and live your life. How you concentrate will also influence how you behave, and the choices you make in both your private and professional life. Yet, ironically, in the twenty-first century, as never before, we now live our lives in ways that conspire to make it increasingly difficult to concentrate. We have evolved a 24/7 lifestyle that means we can work non-stop – even when we're on holiday – and we expect to multitask persistently, in order to try to achieve more and more. The downside of all this relentless activity is that our ability to concentrate, and to concentrate well in a way that achieves satisfying results, is becoming eroded, and this means we can end up achieving less, rather than more.

Think of all the labour-saving gadgets and devices we own today, compared to what we had a hundred years ago. Sometimes, especially if you take a step back, it can feel as though the things we have in our lives that are supposed to save us time and effort – from washing machines to word processors – are doing just the opposite and actually creating more for us to do. Where, once, we would have known and accepted that a particular job would require a reasonable amount of time to complete successfully we now expect to do everything more quickly, do it more and do it right now. When emails can be answered at any time of day or night, from an inconspicuous hand-held object the size of a pack of cards, we have no reason to ever stop work. However, what more and more people are discovering is that these increasing demands can make work more difficult, not easier, as the brain struggles to work concurrently on a multitude of tasks. Because of our hyperactive, overstimulated approach, which serves to inhibit concentration rather than aid it, we can paradoxically end up achieving less.

Persistent interruptions affect intelligence

Research carried out in 2005 by psychologist Dr Glenn Wilson at London's Institute of Psychiatry found that the persistent interruptions and distractions in the office had quite an effect on workers. The study found that excessive use of technology actually reduced their intelligence, and those distracted by emails and phone calls saw a ten-point fall in their IQ, which is twice that found in studies of the impact of smoking marijuana. More than half of the 1,100 study participants said they always responded to an email 'immediately' or as soon as possible, while 21 per cent admitted that they would interrupt a meeting to do so. Those who were constantly breaking away from tasks to react to email or text messages were suffering similar adverse effects on the mind as those caused by losing a night's sleep, said Wilson. While new technologies can undoubtedly increase productivity (when used judiciously), when the use of them was unchecked these constant disruptions were found to be reducing workers' acuity, and consequently their ability to work well.

Time to slow down

The brain is a wonderfully effective organ, but are we working against it, rather than with it, in our efforts to achieve more? Increasingly, levels of multitasking suggest we are, and we are now beginning to see the results of this: increased stress and mental health problems, disruptive schoolchildren, burnout, physical problems from obesity to arthritis and a frenzied approach to our everyday lives. From gym classes at 5.00 a.m. to 'speed yoga' (surely a contradiction in terms?), while we rely on food supplements instead of nutritious meals, some supposedly therapeutic activities actually serve to exacerbate the problem rather than alleviate it: taking ginkgo biloba rather than a walk in the park just isn't enough to compensate for an over-extended lifestyle.

When journalist and social commentator Carl Honoré published his book *In Praise of Slow* in 2005, it was in recognition of the fact that we are all moving too fast for our own good. He says:

> It seems to me that we are moving towards an historical turning point. For at least 150 years, everything has been getting faster, and for the most part, speed was doing us more good than harm in that time. But in recent years, we've entered the phase of diminishing returns. Today we are addicted to speed, to cramming more and more into every minute. Every moment of the day feels like a race against the clock, a dash to a finish line that we never seem to reach. This roadrunner culture is taking a toll on everything from our health, diet and work to our communities, relationships and the environment.

The Slow Movement began in Italy with food, but is beginning to seep into all aspects of life, and with it comes the rewards of taking time to concentrate on what you are doing – which will, inevitably, increase your focus and enjoyment. It doesn't matter what you are doing – taking a walk, writing an essay, cooking a meal, making love: you will get more out of all these activities with a little more concentration.

But it's not easy. All those speedy hormones that we generate just from day-to-day living are highly addictive. We actually find it hard to stop and just sit still, thinking or contemplating anything from a piece of music to a shopping list. Relaxing feels unnatural. Doing just one thing at a time feels odd. Music, for example, has increasingly become a background noise, rather than something to be relished and savoured. Fast food implies that eating is a time-wasting activity, something to be done while doing something else – working at your desk, maybe? And with these persistent bad habits, we put our ability to concentrate at risk.

Effect on relationships

We also put our relationships at risk. Children who spend hours isolated in their rooms, communicating with their peers only via MSN, text or internet gaming, are losing out on learning the social cues gleaned from non-verbal communication. Given that an estimated 93 per cent of communication is non-verbal and gained through subconscious observation of body language, missing opportunities to interact with friends in person is a huge developmental loss. Family meals, once an opportunity to share the day's events in a relaxed and congenial way, are increasingly a thing of the past as grabbing a snack between activities becomes the norm. Extra-curricular activities, to which many children are endlessly shepherded in an effort to maximize their experience of all social, sporting and cultural activities that could improve their future prospects, allow little possibility for the sort of downtime that refreshes and restores the brain. If children are unable to have this, those future prospects will become less, rather than more, possible. Stressed children just cannot make the sort of progress that their over-zealous parents might wish.

And that's just the children, never mind the adults. How many couples have you seen at dinner, joined by that unwelcome third guest, the BlackBerry, which leaves one person seething with resentment as the other taps away, distracted and more interested in what their emails have to say. Or the mobile phone – 'I just have to take this call, darling: it might be work' – interrupting time spent together, with the implication that work is more important than concentrating on them.

A study on communication overload, commissioned by British Gas in the UK in 2004, flagged the emerging emphasis on communication technologies, and the detrimental effect this was having on human relationships. Since then we now also have to contend with blogging and twittering that are so easy to access via a BlackBerry or iPhone. Back then, nearly four hours a day was being spent on communicating with others – but via phone, texting and emailing, not in person. And even though people are keeping in touch in electronic ways, the study found that this didn't actually improve communication about what really matters. Of the 1,105 people interviewed, one in five said they didn't know what was going on in their loved ones' lives, or how they were feeling. 'When we see people face-to-face we really invest in the relationship, but it's becoming so simple to keep in touch in other ways, why make the time?' says Cary Cooper, professor of organizational psychology and health at Lancaster University Management School, when commenting on the study. How much worse has the overuse of communication technologies become since then?

Becoming absorbed in a private cyberworld is also a way of shutting out others, and seems almost addictive. 'There's something quite compelling about contemporary gadgetry', said relationships counsellor Martin Lloyd-Elliot, in a feature in *The Times* in 2009. 'These new designs seem to activate part of the brain that wants to be absolutely absorbed and, like computer games, they can create a strange altered state in the user, in which he or she is with you but not available to you.' In 2008, it was reported that Madonna and Guy Ritchie, whose relationship ended in divorce, slept with their BlackBerrys under their pillows. 'It's not unromantic,' she said, 'it's practical.' Six months later they'd separated. You have been warned: concentrate on your BlackBerry rather than your partner at your peril.

Harnessing the brain

In recent years, our brain and how it works have come under increasing scrutiny. True, the full extent of the brain's ability is not yet known, and we believe it has endless capacity, but we're also beginning to understand more about some of its limitations. With the advent of fMRI scanning (functional Magnetic Resonance Imaging scans), which can show, in real time, the different areas of the brain that are activated when confronted with specific thought processes such as doing a maths problem or listening to music, or even just feeling happy, scientists, psychologists and doctors are learning more and more about what we are capable of – and what we can do to improve these capabilities.

Psychologist Peter Clough, a lecturer at Hull University who is working on mental toughness with pupils at All Saints Catholic High School in Merseyside, believes he can boost students' grades by improving their mental toughness. He uses games that train them to concentrate and focus, one of which is Mindball. This is a game where the goal is to be more relaxed than your opponent and, by concentrating hard, move a ball along a tabletop. The players wear headbands with electrodes that are connected to the table, and the electrodes are wired to a biosensor system. The same system that is used to measure the body's biological signals registers the electrical activity in the brain, an electroencephalogram (EEG): this is an electrical waveform that is recorded from the brain by using electrodes placed on the head. By concentrating well and relaxing, the player influences his or her brain waves in a way that makes the ball move. The most successful player is the one who is concentrating best. The headteacher at the school, Peter Bradley, says that practising these skills boosts students' powers of concentration, resilience and confidence – and this will help them with their exams. The beauty of games like Mindball is that the teenagers can see for themselves how they can manage their own thoughts and improve their levels of concentration, which in turn helps self-confidence.

A study conducted by London's Imperial College demonstrated that EEG feedback, as used in the Mindball game, can definitely improve academic performance and creativity. Once the basic ability to focus and relax has been achieved, the player can increase the sensitivity level to achieve even higher states of relaxation and concentration.

The importance of our natural environment

There is so much that we can do to improve our ability to concentrate, but one of the first steps we can take is to recognize how difficult we can make it for ourselves. Even the environment in which we live can make a difference, as research into the impact of city life has shown. 'The mind is a limited machine', warns Marc Berman, a psychologist at the University of Michigan in the US, and lead author of a study published in 2009 that measured the cognitive deficits caused by a short urban walk. 'And we're beginning to understand the different ways that a city can exceed those limitations.' In Berman's research with undergraduates at the University of Michigan, some of the students took a walk around an arboretum, while others walked the busy streets. The volunteers were then subjected to a range of psychological tests. Those who had walked through the city were in a worse mood and scored significantly lower in a test of attention and working memory; even looking at a photograph of urban scenes, when compared with looking at pictures of nature, led to measurable impairments. 'We see the picture of the busy street, and we automatically imagine what it's like to be there', explains Berman. 'And that's when your ability to pay attention starts to suffer.' These findings could help explain why children with attention deficit disorders have fewer symptoms in more natural, rural settings. When surrounded by trees and animals, they are less likely to have behavioural problems and are better able to focus on a particular task.

This knowledge is borne out by work done by the environmental psychologist Professor Stephen Kaplan, also from the University of Michigan, who coined the term 'attention restoration theory' or ART, which is concerned with ways of restoring the brain's equilibrium and its ability. He defined this theory as

> . . . an analysis of the kinds of environments that lead to improvements in directed-attention abilities. Nature, which is filled with intriguing stimuli, modestly grabs attention in a bottom-up fashion, allowing top-down directed-attention abilities a chance to replenish. Unlike natural environments, urban environments are filled with stimulation that captures attention dramatically and additionally requires directed attention (e.g. to avoid being hit by a car), making them less restorative. We present two experiments that show that walking in nature or viewing pictures of nature can improve directed-attention abilities, as measured with a backwards digit-span task and the Attention Network Task, thus validating Attention Restoration Theory.

Kaplan's work suggests that the relentless need we have in an urban environment to monitor our surroundings – avoiding other pedestrians on a crowded pavement, trying to cross a busy intersection safely, looking in shop windows, responding to noise from traffic, conversations, iPods – puts us on high alert and demands the sort of hyper-vigilance (the brain monitoring for potential threats to our safety) that isn't needed in a more tranquil place. Yes, it can be exciting and stimulating and, in short bursts, possibly helps keep us on our intellectual toes, but if it's the only environment in which we operate, the constant act of paying attention to this bombardment of peripheral and distracting information may come at a price: it takes energy and effort, and it consumes much of the brain's processing power to stay on high alert. It's also stressful, and the release of stress hormones depletes the brain's resources. Recognizing the impact of an urban environment on our brains, and taking steps to reduce it – even if this is just taking your lunch in a park – can go a long way to helping restore attention.

The link between mind and body

Acknowledging the link between the body and the mind, and vice versa, is increasingly becoming the norm, and it is integral to the work of French psychiatrist Dr David Servan-Schreiber. 'The emotional brain controls everything that governs one's psychological well being, as well as what governs a large part of the body's physiology: the working order of the heart, blood pressure, hormones, the digestive system and even the immune system', he writes in his best-selling book *Healing Without Freud or Prozac*. Servan-Schreiber identifies a number of key features of ensuring the sort of emotional well-being that can only give us an advantage and that we should ignore at our peril: getting 'high' on exercise, maximizing our intake of omega-3s (see page 46), addressing painful memories, waking up to the sun (keeping regular hours), practising heart coherence (see page 216) and seeking a larger connection in life.

So we know what detracts from our ability to concentrate, but what's it going to take before we recognize how essential it is that we pause, take stock of our lives and improve the way in which we operate, allowing for the possibility of better concentration? Do we wait until we hit burnout or break down, or some slip of concentration puts our life, or those of others, at risk? Failing an exam is one thing; failing to see a pedestrian on a zebra crossing is another. And is our constant, stressful, unfocused activity also putting us at risk of degenerative brain diseases such as Alzheimer's, as Dr Dharma Singh Khalsa, president and medical director of the Alzheimer's Research and Prevention Foundation in Tucson, Arizona, suggests? From his work on brain longevity, he believes that the stress hormone cortisol is a causative factor in brain degeneration. 'Cortisol robs your brain of its only source of fuel: glucose', he writes in his book *The Mind Miracle*. 'It also wreaks havoc on your brain's chemical messengers – your neurotransmitters – which carry your thoughts from one brain cell to the next. When your neurotransmitter function is disrupted, and when your brain's fuel supply plummets, it's difficult for you to concentrate and remember.'

You can make a difference

The good news is that you can make a difference. You can decide to do things differently, and improve both your concentration levels and your quality of life in the process. Your brain is open to change, and once it is given a more effective way to work, it will work better. In all areas of life, from work productivity to relationships, from leisure time to your health, you can only benefit. But like any 'muscle', the ability to concentrate has to be exercised. Initially, concentrating may seem like a discipline but then it will become a way of life and, once integrated, the new habits it involves – turning off the BlackBerry when you finish work, shutting down MSN while you concentrate on a book, listening to music to the exclusion of all else, doing nothing but sitting with your child while they play so that you can talk to them – will reap their own rewards. This is less about mental callisthenics and more about balance – work that brain as hard as you like, but do it one task at a time and take time out afterwards to recover. While there is a huge amount of scientific knowledge about the brain that can be utilized and worked with, to concentrate is an art – and one that can be revisited and learned. Everything we've learned about training our bodies – from nutrition to exercise to relaxation – can be applied to the art of concentration. And if you want the benefits of a more productive, more balanced and more effective life, then learning the art of concentration is definitely worth your time, attention and consideration.

CHAPTER ONE
How the brain develops

If the human brain were so simple that we could understand
it, we would be so simple that we couldn't.

Emerson M. Pugh

That's why you develop a brain, so you can think
about more than one thing at a time.

Bill Clinton

I t's worth taking the time to review how the brain works and
evolves from birth, as its influence, and the influences on
it, all interplay and can have an effect on our ability – or
lack of – to concentrate. Although there may be an art to concentration, harnessing the brain's capacity and capability, and
understanding what can affect these, underpins this art.

Your brain is amazing
In simple terms, the brain is a bundle of interconnected neurons. These are highly specialized cells, capable of conducting
information, which enable the brain to perform or control an
astonishingly wide range of complex functions, from simple

physical movements like the blink of an eye to abstract thought processes. At birth, almost all the brain's neurons are present – around 100 billion of them – but the brain is not yet full sized; by the age of four, the brain is 95 per cent of adult size, and by adolescence, the brain is fully grown, if not yet fully mature. This maturation process goes on until the late teens or early twenties.

It is in response to external stimulation that the brain develops, and forms the persistent linking-up of connections and interconnections between the neurons. At birth, a baby's brain looks quite smooth in contrast to the wrinkled appearance of a more mature brain, which has developed as a result of this stimulation of the senses. The environment in which a child grows up greatly influences motor, visual and spatial development, language acquisition, emotional control and other abilities – irrespective of the genetic material a child is born with, although this too will play its part.

Our knowledge of the brain and how it works is still a work in progress, but a lot of what we do now know was gleaned from research into the effects of trauma or disease, and how these affect different areas of the brain. One famous case was that of Phineas Gage who, in 1848, was packing explosives when a charge accidentally blew a 3cm-wide iron bar through his skull. The bar entered just below the eye and exited through the top of his head. Astonishingly, not only did he survive, but he also walked to find a doctor to help him. Although he then collapsed into a coma and suffered meningitis, he eventually recovered, but his personality was completely changed. This led to the initial hypothesis that the area of his brain that had been damaged in the accident was responsible for higher intellectual functioning. Early neurologists tended to pursue their discoveries on the back of relating different areas of brain damage to particular areas of function.

Over time, non-invasive scanning devices like X-rays, EEG (electroencephalogram), CT (computed tomography) scans, PET (positron emission tomography) scans, SPECT (single photo emission tomography) scans and MRI (magnetic resonance imaging) scans have been developed, which can be used to show the brain's activity in a conscious person. Researchers can use these devices to test which areas of the brain show increased activity when a conscious person performs a specific task, such as solving maths puzzles, and these studies have helped us to understand better how the brain works.

Just as important, and becoming increasingly better understood, is the effect of positive attention – love, if you like – on the development of not only the brain's function but also its social-emotional abilities, how the two are interconnected and how they influence each other. Social-emotional ability and emotional intelligence are increasingly being recognized as playing a crucial role in the way people function.

In terms of its basic organization, the brain is divided into four main areas: the brain stem, the cerebellum, the limbic system and the cortex. The brain stem concerns itself with the basic, automatic functions of the body that we do without thinking – the regulation of our breathing, heart rate, blood pressure and digestive system, for example – while the top of the brain stem, called the mid-brain, is responsible for numerous sensory and motor functions such as eye movement. The cerebellum is only one tenth of the brain's size but is made up of around half of all its neurons. Its primary function is to coordinate movement and balance, which means that it must process huge amounts of information from other areas of the body and the brain, and pass it on.

The limbic system of the brain, nestling above the brain stem and between the two halves of the cortex, is home to the thalamus and the hypothalamus, the basal ganglia, the amygdala and the hippocampus. The thalamus is the gateway through which all sensory information from the body (apart from the nose) and the information from the cerebellum is processed. It also acts as a sort of relay station, passing on any information to the cortex for any further conscious processing that may be necessary. Below the thalamus is the hypothalamus, which is connected to almost every part of the brain and controls numerous critical functions, including hormone regulation and the balancing of a multitude of physical processes including our individual circadian rhythms. The basal ganglia is vital for the coordination of fine motor control – the ability of the body to make precise and controlled movements – and is damaged by diseases like Parkinson's.

The amygdala has a crude 'fight or flight' response which allows us to short-circuit the cortex when necessary and react instinctively to perceived danger. When you see a sudden movement out of the corner of your eye and flinch to move away from potential damage, that's your amygdala working. It is initially primitive in its reaction, but has an additional and significant role in generating emotional responses, and affects our social adaptation.

The amygdala also scans everyday experiences for their motivational significance, linked to the reward of pleasurable sensation. This can be relevant in creating positive outcomes from the process of concentrating on something – whether this is mastering a piece of music or a video game. The hippocampus has an important role in forming memories: it takes experiences and creates new neural pathways, storing information for future reference, forming the basis of our long-term memories and retrieving information when necessary. The olfactory bulb is also in the limbic system, and stores information received from our noses – which is why smells can be so evocative, bringing memories flooding back. With its links with emotions, motivation, memory and pleasure, the limbic system has a part to play in both the ability to concentrate and to be distracted from concentration.

The cortex forms the most obvious part of the brain, the two hemispheres that sit at the top and are joined together by a thick bundle of nerve fibres called the *corpus callosum*, through which information between the two passes backwards and forwards. This is the 'grey matter' sometimes referred to when talking about the brain. Grey matter consists of six layers of highly specialized neurones that reach down to the white matter both within the cortex and extending into other areas of the brain and create an extensive interconnecting network of neurones. This rapid-fire connectedness is what allows the complex process of thought.

The two hemispheres of the cortex are divided into four main areas, or lobes: the frontal, parietal, occipital and temporal lobes. The frontal lobe, located behind the forehead, is concerned with what is often termed the 'executive function' of the brain. This describes our capacity to do more than one thing at a time, plan future tasks, direct our attention, control impulsive behaviour – in short, manage and organize what the rest of the brain does. The occipital lobes process information received via the eyes, converting this into images we understand, while the temporal lobes are concerned primarily with language and sound. The parietal lobes also process sensory information, particularly spatial and visual perception.

All this interconnectedness doesn't happen overnight. The brain evolves only through stimulation and the use it receives, and while there are definite phases of activity this is quite a linear process: stimulation, experience and usage create its ability. Studies with children who have been understimulated – for example, babies abandoned in Romanian orphanages, many of whom were very badly neglected – show restricted brain development. Interestingly, studies have also shown that geniuses seem to be made, not born. Researchers now know that it is the constant practising of an activity that leads to excellence, and studies show that this process takes roughly 10,000 hours. 'In study after study, of composers, basketball players, fiction writers, ice-skaters, concert pianists, chess players, this number comes up again and again', says neuroscientist Daniel Levitin, professor of psychology and behavioural neuroscience at McGill University in Montreal, Canada. 'Ten thousand hours is equivalent to roughly three hours a day, or 20 hours a week, of practice over 10 years. No one has yet found a case in which true world-class expertise was accomplished in less time. It seems that it takes the brain this long to assimilate all that it needs to know to achieve true mastery.' So even if there is a genetic predisposition towards an area of talent or excellence, without putting in the practice time, this potential will never be realized.

Whether or not achieving true mastery is the objective, whatever we want to achieve we have to give the brain time and practice, and in order to do this, we need to be able to concentrate on the task in hand.

Your brain in utero

Brain development begins almost at the point of conception. Even before the fertilized egg has implanted in the wall of the womb, cell division has been occurring, with the number of cells doubling every twelve hours following the meeting of sperm and ovum. Cells also begin to differentiate, initially between those that will form the embryo and those that will form the placenta. Around seven days after fertilization, the fertilized egg implants in the lining of the womb. Within the cluster of embryonic cells, differentiation continues and three layers of cells emerge. The outer layer becomes the brain, spinal cord and nerves, parts of the eyes and ears, the skin, hair and nails; the middle layer becomes the skeleton, heart and muscles, blood cells, kidneys and other organs; while the inner layer forms the digestive tract, and the respiratory and urinary systems. Within fifteen days – with the embryo still only about a centimetre in diameter – nerve cells begin to form and the brain is activated. Extraordinary to think that for many women all this is happening before they have even missed a period or suspect they are pregnant.

Fortunately the embryo is something of a parasite and will source what it needs to develop from its host. It is also protected by the placenta, which can prevent most, but not all, harmful substances reaching the baby. Substances harmful to the developing baby, called teratogens, include numerous drugs, alcohol, nicotine, cocaine, opiates, marijuana; chemical pollutants like lead, and dioxin; and some bacteria and viruses, particularly rubella and toxoplasmosis. Whether or not a baby is affected by exposure to teratogens will depend on many variables, including levels of exposure and timing – that is, at what point of the baby's development that exposure occurs.

Otherwise, as long as the maternal diet is good, the baby's developing brain should get all the nutritional support it needs. Current wisdom is to supplement the mother-to-be's diet with folic acid, prior to conception and for the first couple of months of pregnancy, to reduce the risk of neural tube defects like spina bifida. Another recommendation for healthy brain development is to ensure an adequate maternal intake of essential fatty acids: omega-3, and in particular DHA, which stands for docosahexaenoic acid, which is used to make brain fats. These can be taken in by eating fatty fish like mackerel several times a week, but where there is a concern about dioxin pollutants, supplementing with a purified supplement form may be preferable.

Over the weeks of pregnancy, averaging around forty for most women, the baby's brain development continues, but it is within the first three months that the hugely important cell differentiation and organization begins and ends. Most development after this time is about maturing and growing, so what happens during the first three months is critical. Sensory awareness also begins in the womb as the ability to see, hear and feel develop. Foetal movements, even if not felt by the mother until about twenty weeks, start as early as eight weeks, and all this activity begins to create rudimentary neural connections. At fifteen weeks, a foetus can respond to external stimuli and develops a startle reflex. He (or she) is not unaffected by his external environment and will recognize his mother's voice, and other familiar sounds, after birth.

The internal environment of the growing foetus can also be influenced by his mother's hormones and her stress hormones, particularly cortisol, can cross the placental barrier. If a mother has an over-sensitized stress response, and habitually produces high levels of cortisol, then this can pass on a similar sensitivity to her baby. A highly stressed pregnant mother can result in a baby born with his stress response set inappropriately high, which could have an influence on all his reactions to life from day one. A study published in the *European Journal of Gynaecology and Reproductive Biology* by Gitau (et al) in 2001 showed evidence of this. The researchers discovered that high cortisol levels transferring from the mother could affect both the developing hypothalamus, responsible for regulating hormones involved in motivation and reward, and the hippocampus, which converts experience into memory, storing it for future use. Having a stress response set too high could also, as a consequence, make concentration difficult. Babies who show signs of hyperarousal find it difficult to focus on one thing for long, needing extra external help in soothing and regulating themselves.

Baby to child

The minute a newborn baby takes his first breath, the sensory impact of life outside the womb continues to create new neural pathways and connections. We know, for example, from animal studies, that if visual stimuli are restricted to only one eye, then the visual cortex related to the other eye won't develop, and even after visual stimuli are reintroduced, vision remains impaired. Seeing bright lights, hearing unmuffled noise, and being touched and held, fed and nourished and responded to with love and warmth, all help the infant brain to develop in a healthy way. Apart from the neurones that will develop over time in the cerebellum and hippocampus, a baby is born with almost all the brain cells he will ever have. However, significantly, what happens during the first year of life is a huge increase in the connections that are made between brain cells, and then a pruning process as the fine tuning of relevant neurones occurs.

For example, at birth even a premature baby can discriminate between male and female voices. Studies have shown that a two-day-old, full-term baby can distinguish between his maternal language and a foreign one, while a three-day-old baby can recognize his mother's voice. Babies are also born with the impressive ability to recognize actual faces, as opposed to seeing only a haphazard arrangement of facial features, and within a few days they know their mothers' faces. This is useful for survival because it ensures they respond to those most regularly seen, and that their caregiver stays close to care for them. Babies under six months old remain good at discriminating between faces, but after this time the process of fine tuning begins, whereby they begin to focus more on what is most relevant to them. You could think of this as a kind of pruning of the neural pathways they no longer need and a strengthening of those pathways that lead to faster, more efficient and more accurate powers of recognition.

Studies have also shown that a baby's brain development will always suffer from a deprived learning environment. In the Romanian orphanages, where babies were grossly neglected in appalling conditions, it was shown that poor nutrition, ill health and, crucially, little or no sensory stimulation all had a devastating effect on the development of walking and talking skills, and seriously impaired the children's social, emotional and cognitive development. Research carried out by Michael Rutter at the University of London showed a close link between the length of time of deprivation and the extent of intellectual impairment, and while some babies made an extraordinary recovery when given continued and excellent remedial care, there were some who continued to show evidence of autistic-like behaviour.

For most babies the nurturing environment of normal family life is more than stimulating and secure enough to ensure they develop normally.

The adolescent brain

All things being equal, healthy children grow and develop in a straightforward manner, happy to fit in with their families. And then they hit adolescence, leaving many parents wondering what has happened to their equable, biddable, life-enjoying offspring and where this new entity has come from, often seemingly overnight. While it is easy to dismiss the whole process in a single word – hormones – it is worth considering what this phase actually consists of, especially as it usually coincides with a critical period in education. It is profoundly distressing to a lot of parents that at a time when they would like their child to concentrate on school work, they seem incapable of concentrating on anything, indulging instead in thoughtless, demotivated and risk-taking activity. Why?

Up until the 1960s, it was generally thought that the brain was fully mature by adolescence. Then work done by Dr Peter Huttenlocher, a neurologist at the University of Chicago Child Hospital in the US, showed that there were two main changes in the brain before and after puberty. In the first year of life, there is a huge proliferation of brain cells, and the connections made between them, and at this point, the capacity for connections – synapses – between the brain cells is at its most dense; then those that aren't used begin to get 'pruned', while those that are used begin to strengthen. In the frontal lobe, however, this proliferation continues without pruning throughout childhood. Then, after puberty, while brain volume itself does not change, there is an increase in white matter in the frontal cortex, caused by an increase in myelin – the fatty tissue that appears white under a microscope, making the cells look less grey – which is responsible for insulating and protecting brain cells, and allowing for even faster transmission of activity in the frontal cortex. Also after puberty there is a vigorous 'pruning' in the frontal cortex, and because this is important for fine tuning, and the frontal cortex is responsible for executive planning – our capacity to do more than one thing at a time, plan future tasks, direct our attention, control impulsive behaviour – the combination of increased myelination and fine tuning helps the brain mature. Eventually. In the meantime, the brain is a work in progress and the executive ability to link cause and effect, in particular, seems to be unreliable. Adolescent behaviour, particularly in boys, seems to overlook the very obvious (to the rest of us) fact that if you leap out of a second-floor window, for example, you might break your leg.

With this increased activity in the frontal cortex, there is also an increase the sort of self-conscious, self-absorbed and selfish behaviour that is so characteristic of adolescents. There is another consequence of this remodelling of the cortex, which is what is happening here, that can make teenagers seem so insensitive to other people. This is a reduced ability to recognize other people's emotions. Research studies, based on showing adolescents pictures of facial expressions, showed that they are 20 per cent less likely to read them accurately, making them socially inept. Further research, using MRI scans while adolescents were looking at faces on a computer screen, carried out in the US by Dr Deborah Yurgelun-Todd at Harvard's McLean Hospital, showed that the amygdala area of young teens' brains was activated during this activity, utilizing a more immediate but less reasoned gut reaction. Older teens showed greater activity in their frontal lobes, demonstrating a more considered and accurate identification of the emotions depicted.

So the behaviour of adolescents tends to be impulsive, they misread facial expressions and have no appreciation of how others feel, and this is before you throw hormones into the mix. But it's not just the hormones – testosterone in boys and oestrogen in girls – that creates problems. There is also an increase in production of melatonin, and a biological shift in their sleep needs – hence the characteristically adolescent pattern of staying up half the night and not getting up until noon. Not only do they have an increased need for sleep, but they also suffer the equivalent of jet lag, and many end up chronically sleep deprived, with all the added impact that this has on their behaviour – moodiness, irritability and being reactionary.

The adult brain

So it would seem that by early adulthood, the brain is fully mature and functional, and you might think the story of brain development ends there, but something that is relevant in late adolescence is also relevant in the adult brain: plasticity. Plasticity is described as the ease with which connections are made between neurons, and how these connections are modified in response to how often they are used.

Neuroplasticity refers to the continued changes that can occur in the brain as the result of exposure to new experiences and learning opportunities, referred to by neurologists as 'experience-dependent plasticity'. This has been seen to occur after injury to the brain, where plasticity allowed new functional and structural changes to take place to compensate for the damaged area. This is what makes rehabilitation so important, and creates the possibility for regaining some, if not all, previously damaged brain function.

It was previously thought that the adult brain was hard wired and no longer capable of new development. It had been thought that after critical periods of development there would be no more change and that the sensory pathways were fixed, even while areas like the hippocampus – concerned with processing memory – continued to produce new neurons. It seems, however, that if exposed to enough opportunities, we go on learning, process what we learn and apply that learned experience – all of which encourages the formation of new neurons in the hippocampus.

Research carried out on taxi-drivers' brains by a team of neuroscientists at University College London, and published in *The Lancet* in 2000, showed this process of plasticity. London taxi drivers have to learn huge amounts of information and

◎ EXERCISE YOUR MEMORY

Get into the habit of remembering, and recalling, important phone numbers. Your own phone number is easily remembered, but learn and remember those of your closest relatives and friends – and your mobile phone number – without constantly looking it up. Then try learning and remembering your credit card details. Of course, you can keep phone numbers written down, but making the effort to learn strings of numbers, which have meaning for you, will also help you remember other important numbers like your PIN.

manage to retain a vast knowledge of the spatial arrangement of the city via a redistribution of grey matter in the hippocampus of the brain. The researchers compared 16 male taxi drivers with 50 men who didn't drive taxis, and found that the posterior hippocampus, linked previously with navigational skills, was significantly larger in the taxi drivers.

Further research done in the US by Hongjun Song at Johns Hopkins University School of Medicine in 2007, on new cell formation in the hippocampus in mice, confirms earlier findings about plasticity. Not only did the new cells created by new experiences (in a process known as neurogenesis) show a greater degree of activity than the older cells, but they were also able to integrate into existing brain circuits and modify them. 'This indicates that adult neurogenesis continuously provides a pool of highly excitable and flexible neurons facilitating the formation of new connections within the adult brain', says Josef Bischofberger, a neuroscientist at the University of Freiburg in Germany, who commented on the study. 'At the same time, maturation will slowly "cool down" the new cells making them reliable units for stable representation and storage of the newly learned memories.'

Because of their plasticity, newly generated neurons increase the plasticity of the old networks, by modifying them to incorporate new information. Older cells then accommodate and adapt to the new conditions, improving their function. What is also known is that exercise increases the formation of new neurons in the hippocampus, and this, in turn, leads to better memory performance.

Not only is adult brain development shaped by external stimuli, but it also coincides with the busiest time of our lives. Most adults have to become adept at multitasking, juggling careers and families, and while we are probably at the peak of our mental and physical powers during this life stage, overload and burnout are frequently the price many of us pay for this business. These can not only affect our performance but can also store up stress-related health problems for later life.

Recent research has shown that it is possible to generate and regenerate brain cells throughout life. However, doing this is a case not just of improving memory – for example by exercising the area of the brain responsible for memory – but also of enhancing the senses, because unless what we see, hear or feel is processed accurately, then the brain cannot process or store information as well as it once did. Understanding more about the links between sensory perception, memory and cognition has enabled scientist to work out what exercises will help brain plasticity.

The basic scientific principles for brain plasticity are:
○ Keep learning new activities that link and challenge both your physical and mental ability.
○ Choose activities that start relatively easy and progress, keeping you at the threshold of challenge.
○ Engage different processing systems in the brain.
○ Make accomplishing each progressive step its own reward.
○ Keep things novel and surprising to help increase focus.

◉ USE IT OR LOSE IT

Whatever your age, but perhaps most importantly as you move into old age, choose activities that help plasticity. Here are some examples:

○ **Learn to dance** – whether it's the cha-cha, line dancing or the waltz, something with form and rules that will make you concentrate mentally on doing something physically.

○ **Try a new physical activity like juggling** – start with two balls, and progress to four or more – learning to skate or riding a bike.

○ **Learn a musical instrument** – even a recorder is a start – because it's progressive, mentally challenging and physical.

○ **Improve or learn a new language** – brushing up the French you learned at school or tackling something new like Mandarin.

○ **Learn to cook** – even learning new recipes and techniques will engage your brain.

The ageing brain

While there is no doubt that in the Western world we are, on average, living longer, there is also an associated risk of age-related decline in our mental powers. It was once thought that older people lose thousands of brain cells every day, but this has now been contradicted by recent studies. It is true that neurons in some areas of the brain, like the basal forebrain, decrease in number as we age, but most neurons in the cortex are retained, while the hippocampus, if stimulated, is capable of generating new cells until the day we die.

Many of us now understand there is a sense of 'use it, or lose it', but there are some inevitable effects of ageing on the brain that we can't escape, because our bodies are deteriorating too. Our sensory organs – eyes and hearing, in particular – tend to deteriorate as well, and with that decline, we may feel less inclination to expose ourselves to new stimuli. The decline of other body systems will also have a similar effect. Our digestive system, for example, becomes less efficient at absorbing the nutrients we need from the food we eat, while the endocrine system becomes less efficient at responding to hormonal messages. Brain cells are also extremely sensitive to oxygen levels and, with a degree of the arteriosclerosis typical of the ageing blood vessels that supply the brain, there will be a reduced blood flow, which in turn reduces the oxygen supply. A low-level but continuous oxygen deficiency will lead to a decline in neurons.

Without continuous external stimulation, new brain-cell production slows down, leading to less brain plasticity because, as research has shown, the plasticity of new brain cells helps old brain cells function better. As we age, we tend to be exposed less to new experiences, become less active and become less sociable, so our opportunities, unless actively sought, for brain stimulation naturally decline. We are less likely to try new things, so overall our opportunities for external stimuli decrease.

This is quite different to, and separate from, degenerative diseases such as Alzheimer's. With Alzheimer's, commonly considered a disease of memory loss, the leading theory is that degenerative changes in the brain are caused by sticky amyloid plaques and neurofibrillary tangles that destroy neurons, and these create increasing communication deficits within the brain. The forgetfulness that is characteristic of early-stage Alzheimer's is a first sign that the processing of short-term and working memory is becoming impaired. Later, as the level of neuron damage increases, the breakdown of learned experience – for example, how to use a knife and fork – grows until the disease eradicates those abilities. It is gradual, and heartbreaking to witness, and at the last stages the brain's ability to regulate bodily functions such as swallowing also falters. Currently there is no cure, and research shows little evidence of a treatment breakthrough any time soon, although there is some evidence of protective measures that can be taken to support and protect the brain – good nutrition, exercise and relaxation techniques like meditation, for example. Research published in 2009, by the University of South Florida in the US, revealed that drinking the equivalent of five cups of coffee a day helped reverse symptoms of dementia in specially bred mice.

The mice were given the equivalent of five 8oz (227g) cups of coffee a day – about 500mg of caffeine, which is about the same as two cups of 'specialty' coffees such as lattes or cappuccinos from coffee shops, 14 cups of tea or 20 soft drinks. When the mice were tested after two months, those who were given the caffeine performed much better in tests measuring their memory and thinking skills, and performed as well as mice of the same age without dementia, while those drinking plain water continued to do poorly in the tests. In addition, the brains of the mice given caffeine showed almost a 50 per cent reduction in levels of the beta amyloid protein, which forms destructive clumps in the brains of dementia patients, while further tests suggest that caffeine affects the production of both the enzymes needed to produce beta amyloid. It was also found that caffeine suppresses the inflammatory changes in the brain that led to an over-production of beta amyloid. The team, led by Dr Gary Arendash, said that they hoped to start human trials soon.

Other dementias can be caused by lack of oxygen to the brain. Mini-strokes or transient ischaemic attacks (TIAs), for example, can cause mini-infarcts, where areas of brain tissue die and, depending on which area of the brain they occur in, can cause problems related to that area of brain control.

The most notable psychological feature of ageing is short-term memory impairment and the lengthening of response time, which can give rise to anxiety about possible Alzheimer's or other dementias. But when older people are given all the time that they need on tests that are not heavily dependent on school skills, their performance is only slightly poorer than that of young adults. In tests that depend on vocabulary, general information and well-practised activities, they show negligible age-related deterioration. So while both low response times and short-term memory impairment contribute to lower scores on standard tests of intelligence for the elderly, removing the difference that low response times and short-term memory impairment creates, will equal this out. It may also be that a lifetime of learning how to focus and concentrate helps too.

Conclusion

○ **That baby is sizing you up ...** Babies perfect the art of recognizing the faces they depend on for survival in the first six months of life. A child's brain develops as a direct response to external stimulation as younger children begin to learn the art of focus and concentration.

○ **Your teenager can't help it!** The adolescent brain changes dramatically, expanding those pathways that facilitate higher thinking and rapid response and shedding or pruning those connections that are no longer useful. But a teenager is a work in progress and during this transition, the ability to link cause and effect diminishes. Increased activity in the frontal cortex means increased self-consciousness, self-absorption and selfish, insensitive behaviours, but this is just a phase and, as the brain settles into a new maturity, and a greater ability to concentrate on what really matters, the teenager will grow out of it.

○ **Exercise can create new brain cells.** The adult brain can create new neurones and researchers now know that regular exercise is one of the best ways adults of all ages can boost brain power, leading to better memory retrieval, performance and concentration.

○ **Brain plasticity increases with new experiences.** Neurologists use the term 'plasticity' to describe the ease with which connections are made between brain cells and then modified, depending on how often they are used. Neuroplasticity describes the continued changes that can occur in the brain as a result of new experiences and learning opportunities. You can improve focus and concentration by exposing yourself to new learning experiences.

○ **Get out there and learn something new.** Because when you do, you not only increase your brain plasticity but also improve the performance of existing connections, which means you will do what you already know how to do, including concentrating on the task in hand, even better than before.

○ **Give older people time to retrieve and process information.** They'll get there and do just as well as younger folk. In tests that depend on vocabulary, general information and well-practised activities, older people, given time to concentrate and complete the task, show negligible age-related deterioration in their brain functioning.

CHAPTER TWO

What inhibits brain function and concentration?

Times alone are when you can listen to your own mind.
That's something we don't allow ourselves today. I was lucky to
grow up in that generation before mobile phones. It's fascinating
how thought processes today are constantly interrupted.
Although we can communicate faster, we are able to think less
quickly and less clearly because of these interruptions.

Ray Mears

Our 24/7, constantly connected, do-it-now lifestyles can lead to amazing productivity. And we all know that great feeling when it's all coming together, when we're firing on all cylinders, not missing a trick and delivering smart, rational, well-organized results. But for more and more of us, responding constantly to the incessant demands of 24/7 life, without any downtime, is causing problems in the short term as we find it more difficult to relax – and possibly, for many of us, in the longer term too, as this high-octane life becomes 'the norm'. Yes, we all know that our work/life balance has got out of hand, but the by-product of this – grabbing a coffee for breakfast, answering emails at midnight, going to the gym at 6.00 a.m. – is contributing to the rat-on-the-treadmill effect

– so much so that, even when we do take time out, we find it hard to wind down. We might pride ourselves on our ability to multitask, but it's just not possible to juggle relentlessly, every day, all the time, without risking dropping a ball. Maybe it's time to take a look at the whole picture and what is eroding our ability to focus and concentrate.

Understanding brain waves

If you've ever wondered what your brain waves are, what they do and how they might be relevant to concentration, then read on. You are probably more aware of the electrical activity in your brain, which is what brain waves are, than you know. If you are 'firing on all cylinders', then you are probably utilizing your beta waves. If you are half-heartedly watching a film on the television, then your alpha waves are operating. And, if you are driving in a rather unfocused way, and another driver beeps you, you can almost feel the switch from alpha to beta, by way of a small shot of adrenalin!

When you're awake and totally active, your brain waves operate at a level called beta, where they oscillate at around 14 to 30 cycles per second. If your mind relaxes, and you begin to switch off from the external world (as you might when you're daydreaming), your brain-wave patterns are mainly composed of alpha waves, which oscillate at around 8 to 13 cycles per second. When you are relaxing even more, the pattern slows further and can oscillate at around 4 to 7 cycles per second, when the waves are known as theta waves. Waves of less than 4 cycles per second are delta waves.

The beta state is associated with maximum concentration, a heightened alertness and visual acuity, which can be valuable when working but exhausting when sustained for extended periods. Alpha waves mean we are in a place of deep relaxation, while they are also associated with being awake and reasonably alert, allowing us access to the creativity that lies just below the surface of our conscious awareness. Alpha waves are on the same frequency as the Schuman Resonance, the resonant frequency of the earth's electromagnetic field. This is also the place from which meditation can occur. Theta waves characterize a rather elusive and extraordinary twilight state of being, of which we are only usually aware just before we drift off to sleep. Theta waves can produce the sort of vivid waking dreams that may have vivid flashes of imagery, and this is also a state in which we are most receptive to information beyond our conscious awareness. Theta meditation is thought to increase creativity and enhance learning, while awaking intuition and other extrasensory perception skills. Delta waves produce the sort of deep, restorative sleep we need to access every night, not least because they are linked to the release of the growth hormone, responsible for children's growth but beneficial to us all for growth and repair.

Gamma brain waves oscillate at a level higher than even beta waves, at a rate of around 40 times per second, but often at between 26 to 70 times. Some researchers do not distinguish gamma waves as a distinct class but include them in beta waves, so they are not always mentioned alongside general information about brain waves, but they are associated with perception and consciousness. Research has shown that gamma waves are continuously present during what's called low voltage fast neocortical activity (LVFA), which occurs when waking from sleep, during active rapid eye movement (REM) sleep; and during moments when bursts of high-level information processing occur, brain waves reach the gamma state.

Research on gamma waves from the Massachusetts Institute of Technology (MIT) in the US, and published in 2009, showed that gamma waves may have some role in regulating how different stimuli are received – that is, how loud we perceive a noise to be, or how bright a light, which may help support the ability to concentrate. And in another study, MIT neuroscientists found that neurons in the brain's centre of planning and executive function, the prefrontal cortex, fire in unison and send signals to the visual cortex to do the same, generating high-frequency waves that oscillate between these distant brain regions like a vibrating spring. These waves, also known as gamma oscillations, have long been associated with cognitive states like attention, learning and consciousness.

'We are especially interested in Gamma oscillations in the prefrontal cortex because it provides top-down influences over other parts of the brain', explains professor of Neuroscience Robert Desimone, director of the McGovern Institute for Brain Research at MIT. 'We know that the prefrontal cortex is affected in people with schizophrenia, ADHD and many other brain disorders, and that Gamma oscillations are also altered in these conditions. Our results suggest that altered neural synchrony in the prefrontal cortex could disrupt communication between this region and other areas of the brain, leading to altered perceptions, thoughts, and emotions.'

Desimone looked for patterns of neural synchrony in two areas of the brain that are associated with attention: the frontal eye field (FEF) within the prefrontal cortex, and the V4 region of the visual cortex. Two monkeys were trained to watch a monitor displaying multiple objects, and to concentrate on one of the objects when cued. Neural activity from the FEF and the V4 regions of the brain was monitored when the monkeys were either paying attention to the object or ignoring it. When the monkeys first paid attention to the appropriate object, neurons in both areas showed strong increases in activity. What the scientists then found was that, as if connected by a spring, the oscillations in each of the two areas of the brain began to synchronize, one with the other. Analysing the timing of this neural activity, researchers found that the prefrontal cortex became engaged by attention first, followed by the visual cortex, suggesting that the prefrontal cortex commanded the visual region to snap to attention. The delay between the neural activity in these two areas during each wave cycle was indicative of the speed at which signals were travelling from one region to the other – as if the two brain regions were 'talking' to one another.

How the different areas of the brain communicate with each other has long been of scientific interest. Research carried out in the US by Dr Robert Knight, professor of psychology at the Helen Wills Neuroscience Institute at UC Berkeley, and published in 2006, looked at the mystery of how widely separated regions of the cortex, involving billions of cells, link together to coordinate complex activities. Even the answering of a simple question involves areas all over the brain that hear it, analyse it, collect the relevant information, formulate the answer and then coordinate muscles in the face for speech. By measuring electrical activity in the brain, researchers found that the slow, theta waves tune in to the fast, gamma waves that signal the transmission of information between different areas. In this way, areas like the auditory cortex and the frontal cortex, although separated by several inches of cerebral cortex, can coordinate effectively.

'If you are reading something, language areas oscillate in Theta frequency allowing high-gamma-related neural activity in individual neurons to transmit information', says Professor Knight. 'When you stop reading and begin to type, Theta rhythms oscillate in motor structures, allowing you to plan and execute your motor response by way of high Gamma. Simple but effective.'

It also appears from this research that the coupling of high-speed gamma waves, which oscillate at extreme speeds of around 200 times per second, with the lower-speed theta waves could be what gives the brain a way to connect low-level perceptions and actions to high-level goals and intentions.

Working with our brain waves, rather than against them, can be highly effective. We know that the ideal state for concentrated bursts of intellectual activity and application is during phases of beta waves, but we also know that pushing these beyond endurance can be counterproductive. We must have other states – alpha waves, in particular – for creativity. We are designed to work well, but we constantly abuse our innate abilities and then, because we are designed for survival, the body's own built-in defence mechanisms force us to capitulate, possibly by failing, and forcing us to rest and recuperate. Much better to have bursts of sustained, effective activity than to try to work against our physical abilities with endless, unfocused activity, which is why it is so beneficial, physically as well as mentally, to be able to concentrate effectively.

Brain fog

There are numerous things that contribute to poor performance when it comes to being able to concentrate. We expect to relentlessly deliver without any downtime. We expect to function well without proper rest. We expect to be able to think clearly even when surrounded by endless distractions. We think we can multitask and be competent in all our efforts, all the time. We neglect to eat regularly. We forget to drink water. We can't find the time for any regular exercise. And then we wonder why we can't remember a simple telephone number from one moment to the next, or where we left the car keys. This is not likely to be incipient Alzheimer's disease, but such attitudes and behaviour can inhibit the brain's useful functioning and cause long-term problems if we don't take note.

Brain fog accurately describes that feeling that you are trying to think through fog, which makes it difficult to see clearly. It feels a bit like using third gear to drive the car on the motorway: a lot of effort with a lot of straining and not much speed. As if you are functioning on only two rather than six cylinders, to coin another driving metaphor. In addition, it will damage the engine permanently if sustained for long periods.

The brain doesn't function in isolation from the rest of the body. The two are inextricably linked and what's good for your body is also good for your brain. While the brain can function well enough when it is deprived of optimum levels of what it needs, it works better when it's well nourished and rested, so taking care of yourself physically will have a direct bearing on the health of your brain and how it functions. This is particularly important in respect of diet, as when 24/7 demands mean we forget to eat properly or well, over time this lack of good 'brain fuel' will start to show. So whatever your age, it's worth considering how the steps you take now will benefit you not only straight away but in the future too when it comes to using your brain.

Diet – what you eat can make a big difference

When it comes to concentration, what you eat can make all the difference. It's not just a grumbling stomach that can distract you from a particular task: low or see-sawing blood-sugar levels will have a direct effect both on energy levels and on mood and the ability to concentrate. Just as the brain needs adequate fuel to function, so poor nutrition can lead to poor performance.

The brain's primary source of energy is glucose, derived from carbohydrates digested by the body. What the brain likes best is a well-regulated supply, rather than the peaks and troughs that can occur when there are long intervals between eating. This see-sawing effect can also be improved by eating foods with a low GI, or glycaemic index (the rate at which carbohydrates are converted into glucose for use by the body). Low GI foods have a longer digestive period and release more consistent levels of glucose more slowly and over a sustained period. Fluctuating glucose levels can reduce the brain's ability to work efficiently and also contribute to irritability or low-level confusion as you react to these fluctuations, all of which will inhibit good focus and concentration. Foods with a low GI include oats, wholegrains, baked beans (without added sugar) and potatoes, but in the case of potatoes those that are chipped (the fat slows digestion and reduces the glycaemic index) rather than mashed. Foods that provide low GI levels are sometimes referred to as 'complex carbohydrates'. Complex carbohydrates take longer to digest and are usually high in fibre, vitamins and minerals. Examples of complex carbohydrates are wholegrain cereals, vegetables, wholemeal pasta, beans (legumes), or pulses and oats. Simple carbohydrates, such as sugar, honey, fruit and fruit juice, are digested very quickly and have high GI levels.

Eating protein foods also reduces blood-sugar spikes, because the protein helps control the insulin release that is triggered by eating carbohydrates. Eating a bar of chocolate for an energy hit can help, but will create an insulin surge that your body has to deal with and can leave you feeling hungry again, sooner rather than later, so it doesn't provide as sustained an effect as the protein-and-carbohydrate combo you will get from a boiled egg and piece of toast. The effect of food, or lack of it, on concentration and mood is easily seen in children, who cannot manage as well when they are hungry and often express this in grumpiness, but it also affects adults, even if they are more socially adept at masking the effect on their mood, if not on their ability to concentrate.

Protein intake is important not just for stabilizing blood-sugar levels, but also because it provides the amino acids that are crucial building blocks for brain cells and neurotransmitters, which are so important for the biochemical process of thinking. Protein digestion also needs adequate micronutrients, found in vitamins and minerals, to convert amino acids into neurotransmitters, all of which brings us back to the importance of a balanced diet, and that old adage 'feed your brain'.

The UK Department of Health recommends that our diet should include five portions of fruit or vegetables a day. This is considered to be the minimum we should be eating, but very few of us get even that. In Australia the recommendation is for seven a day, and in Greece it's nine a day, while the recommendation from the National Cancer Institute in the US is five a day for children, seven for women and nine portions for men. A portion is roughly equivalent to an apple, a banana, a tablespoon of raisins or other dried fruits, two plums, a dessert-sized bowl of salad leaves, two serving spoons of cooked vegetables, for example peas or broccoli, a 150ml glass of fresh fruit juice or smoothie (only one a day to qualify). So breakfast might be a bowl of cereal with a banana sliced on top, plus a glass of fruit juice; lunch might be hummus and grated carrot on granary bread, with an apple; and dinner might be fresh salmon with spinach and watercress salad, followed by poached plums and custard. It is much easier to make sure you get five a day if you prepare and cook food yourself from fresh ingredients.

The reason why we need a minimum of five portions of fruit and vegetables a day is that this is the only way we can be sure of getting all the vitamins, minerals and fibre we need for good health. We will also get the phytonutrients (chemical compounds that occur naturally in plants) we need, for example carotenoids, flavanoids, isoflavins and lignans. While not essential in themselves, phytonutrients are known to promote health and protect against disease. Foods in their natural form also work synergistically – that is, they are designed to work together to get the most from each other. Some nutrients become more available to us when eaten in conjunction with others. Iron, for example, is more available to us in the presence of vitamin C. It's also much easier to create a balanced diet if we include lots of fruit and vegetables, and they are less fattening than other sources of carbohydrates and fats, while being highly nutritious. Cooking, without overcooking, which means boil or steam vegetables only to the point of softening, also serves to make many of the nutrients more easily available to our digestive systems. So balance raw fruit and vegetables with cooked ones, to make the most of the nutrients available.

Detrimental foods

There's really no such thing as a detrimental food, but there is definitely such a thing as detrimental *quantities* of different food substances. Take sugar. In its natural form it can be used to improve the flavour of lots of different things from fruit to cereals, but the use of convenience and highly processed foods means that our consumption of refined sugar has, over the years, rocketed to around 68 kilos (150lb) per person per year (in 1830, consumption was only about 5 kilos (11lb) a year). The downside of this is not just higher obesity rates, increased diabetes and possible cancer diagnoses, etc., as high rates of sugar consumption also knock out other good nutrients – vitamin B, for example, which is very important for the effective functioning of the nervous system and our brains. Maybe this wouldn't matter if today's life expectancy was only 45, as it was a hundred years ago, but we now all want to live and work longer, and, preferably, enjoy all the benefits of an extended lifespan with fully functioning brains. So it's worth thinking about reducing your overall sugar intake, and not just from specific sugar use. Substitute sugar on your breakfast muesli with a handful of blueberries to sweeten the taste and ensure one of your five-a-day fruit and vegetable intake, for example, but also pay attention to the sugar present in refined and processed foods. Don't use sugar substitutes like aspartame instead, which provides its own toxic load, but opt for agave nectar. This is produced from cactus syrup, is naturally sweeter than honey but has a GI that is four to five times lower.

Salt is another potentially detrimental food substance. Used to enhance flavour, it is not so much the salt you add to your freshly produced food that is the problem, but the salt that creeps into your diet through processed foods. In the UK, the recommendation is for no more than 6g of salt a day, but this is considered high by many doctors, who recommend that we should aim for a much lower maximum of 4g a day. As it is, here in the UK, the average daily intake of salt is actually almost 9g a day, 75 per cent of which comes from processed foods. Check out a tin of Heinz tomato soup – 2.8g a tin, almost half your recommended daily allowance if you finish off a whole tin. A slice of bread can contain as much as 0.5g, so four slices is already providing a third of the recommended daily intake and that's before you've added any sort of butter or filling to a sandwich. Even breakfast cereals have added salt. Salt is a hidden danger because it can cause hardening of the arteries and result in high blood pressure, and when this happens in the brain, it will affect its function. Silent infarcts (death to small areas of brain tissue), transient ischaemic attacks (TIAs) and stroke are all assaults on the brain caused by arterial malfunction, and will damage it. Cutting down your salt intake can help reduce this risk.

The good news is that our ability to taste has a well-documented ability to adapt. Even if you think you have a 'sweet tooth' or enjoy your food highly salted, your sense of taste will adapt to reduced levels of salt or sugar. Over time, food will taste just as good with less.

'Good' foods

Hardly a week goes by without some media fireworks about the next, new 'superfood' – one week it's goji berries, the next it's edamame beans. Sometimes a food is out: for example eggs, which were long thought to be too high in cholesterol to be eaten more than three times a week, although they have now been reinstated as an excellent source of protein and quite safe to eat every day. Take such stories with a (small!) pinch of salt, and keep in mind the three basic principles when it comes to food: fresh, diverse, balanced. Try to eat as much fresh, seasonally relevant foods as you can, and also consider frozen vegetables which, because they were frozen when fresh, count too when it comes to nutritional yield. Make your selection as diverse as you like – so goji berries and edamame beans can be among your choices; and balance protein, carbohydrates, fats, etc. in the appropriate quantities. Buy organic if you like, but be mindful that frozen vegetables may have more vitamins than some 'fresh' organic foods flown halfway round the world which have taken a week to get to your table. Frozen peas, for example, may well have higher levels of vitamin C than those shipped from abroad that have been in transit for over a week before you eat them.

Another reason why a high proportion of fruit and vegetables is recommended is the antioxidants they contain. Oxidation occurs when cells are exposed to oxygen. This is why a cut apple turns brown: this is oxidation occurring before your eyes. Some antioxidants like vitamin C and vitamin E are added to other products as a natural preservative. Copella apple juice in the UK, for example, uses vitamin C to preserve the freshly squeezed apple juice and stop it turning brown. Vitamin E is used in some fish oil supplements to help preserve them – you will see it listed on the product as tocopherol. A by-product of cell metabolism, oxidation creates free radicals, cells that scavenge and can cause damage to other cells, not least the DNA in our body's cells. Eating foods that are high in antioxidants is thought to help reduce oxidation in our bodies as our cells metabolize and, by extension, free-radical damage in the body. Free-radical damage is what makes body cells age and, sometimes, mutate. But it's a constantly fluctuating system, so even if cells are mutating, they usually get dealt with quite adequately by the body's defence system before they become troublesome. If you know the foods you eat can help protect against this process – but let's be clear here, they will never stop the ageing process completely – why wouldn't you choose those foods?

There are a number of foods that are particularly high in antioxidants (as well as numerous other nutritious goodies like vitamins and minerals), so you may want to include them regularly in your diet to help keep your brain sharp:

○ **Berries** Raspberries, strawberries, acai berries, goji berries, cranberries, blueberries. Berries contain anthocyanidins, a powerful antioxidant.
○ **Tomatoes** These contain the antioxidant lycopene, which becomes more potent through cooking.

○ **Broccoli** This is a particularly rich source of glucosinolates (also found in other vegetables like cabbage, cauliflower, kale and Brussels sprouts), which the body breaks down into sulphoraphane, a useful antioxidant. Unfortunately, it is also responsible for the sort of flatulence associated with eating cabbage and sprouts.

○ **Carrots** These – and other yellow-orange vegetables like sweet potatoes – contain carotenoids. Cooked carrots yield more of this antioxidant than raw ones, as the cooking process helps make the active ingredient more digestible.

○ **Spinach** Lutein is the antioxidant in spinach and it is particularly good for the health of the eyes.

○ **Onions** Quercetin is found in onions – and also apples, red wine (which also contains another antioxidant, called resveratrol) and black tea – and is a subgroup of the antioxidant flavonoids.

○ **Turmeric** This orange-coloured spice, which is added to a great deal of Indian food, contains the anti-inflammatory and antioxidant chemical curcumin, which has been found to clear amyloid proteins (which cause Alzheimer's disease) injected into the brains of mice.

○ **Tea** While black tea contains theaflavins, green tea contains catechins. Both are potent antioxidants. And white tea is thought to be an even more potent source of antioxidants.

○ **Wholegrains** Wholegrains contain vitamin E, an antioxidant, but are also rich in phytic acid, another potent antioxidant. Used for breads, breakfast cereals and pastas, these are easy to include in the diet.

Food supplements

The key message about supplements, which is always worth re-peating, is that they should be used to supplement a good diet, not to compensate for a poor one. If you are eating nutritiously inadequate foods, or relying on a lot of highly processed or

◎ KEEP A FOOD DIARY FOR A WEEK

So you know what you're supposed to be doing when it comes to feeding your brain, but are you doing it? One of the simplest ways to assess this is to keep a food diary for a week. We often get into eating habits that don't serve us well, and keeping a food diary will immediately give you an overview of how good your general diet is or where you might want to make some simple changes that will improve things straight away.

For example, your daily intake may look a bit like this:

- **Breakfast** – an apple, cup of black instant coffee with two sugars
- **Mid-morning** – can of cola, packet of crisps
- **Lunch** – tuna and salad sandwich, packet of crisps, bar of chocolate, can of cola
- **Mid-afternoon** – cup of instant coffee with two sugars, three biscuits
- **Supper** – takeaway chicken curry, rice, poppadoms, three lagers, coffee with two sugars
- **Bedtime snack** – bowl of sugared cereal, milk

You can immediately see that if replicated throughout the week, your food intake will be very low in fruit and vegetables and complex carbohydrates, and high in sugars and other 'empty' calories. Its nutritional value will be low, and there will be little to keep the body or brain happy.

Here's a revised daily intake that will immediately improve nutritional levels, and will help create some positive change just by cutting out the fizzy drinks:

- **Breakfast** – sugar-free muesli with grated apple and skimmed milk, cup of freshly made coffee
- **Mid-morning** – glass of fresh fruit juice and a small bag of nuts and raisins

▶

○ **Lunch** – tuna and salad sandwich, packet of crisps, banana and two glasses of water

○ **Mid-afternoon** – three oatcakes with honey, glass of water, cup of green tea

○ **Supper** – homemade chicken and spinach curry, rice, stewed apricots and yoghurt; two lagers

○ **Bedtime snack** – glass of milk

junk food, and think that taking nutritional supplements will protect your health, think again. There is a huge market out there for vitamin and mineral supplements, but these should be considered only after first making sure that your diet is as good as you can make it. Far better to spend your money on the freshest ingredients that you can afford than to spend it on expensive supplements. It is always better to get your nutrients from food, rather than supplements, if you can. A diverse diet of different foods will provide you with micronutrients that work together to aid absorption. A poor diet, even with supplements, cannot be as effective when it comes to good nutrition; also you will not get the other components of food that you need – for example roughage, necessary for a properly functioning digestive system.

If you have some reason to think that you or a family member might have a particular deficiency, then it's better to get expert advice from a properly trained and qualified dietician, who will consider your health and lifestyle and make recommendations about those before suggesting supplementation, should it be necessary. Ask your doctor to refer you to a state-registered dietician for advice, rather than seek out someone who has done an unaccredited nutrition course. Too many 'experts' advise nutritionally extreme diets while prescribing expensive supplements.

WHAT SUPPLEMENTS ARE GOOD FOR YOUR BRAIN?

The health columns in newspapers, magazines and websites are awash with recommendations for brain-boosting supplements from St John's wort for Seasonal Affective Disorder (SAD) and mild depression, to ginkgo biloba for improving blood circulation in the brain. However, before you even begin to consider supplementation, it's important to look at your diet. If you suffer from iron-deficiency anaemia, which can make you feel very tired, lethargic and unable to concentrate (and many women of childbearing age are anaemic without realizing it), you may need an iron supplement in the short term. But there is no point taking an iron supplement without reviewing what is currently lacking in your diet to have caused this. Often people will take a supplement as a precaution, rather than thinking about what it is they are hoping to achieve, and without fully understanding its implications. So certainly consider a supplement if you feel like you need a bit of a boost, but do so only in the context of your overall diet and think about how improving it might be of greater benefit in the long run.

OMEGA-3 EFAS

The one nutritional supplement that shows up, time and again, as having a clinically proven positive impact on brain function is omega-3 essential fatty acid (EFA). Not all EFAs can help support brain function. It must be, specifically, an omega-3 fatty acid.

Ignore the recommendation to supplement your diet with omega-6. Omega-6 fatty acids already exist extensively in our diet – they are available from vegetable oils and cereal-fed animal fats – and so do not need to be taken in supplement form. In fact, some doctors and scientists believe that the excessive amounts of omega-6 already available in our diet may be contributing to the increase in cellular inflammation that could be linked to increased rates of arthritis, depression and Alzheimer's disease. Ideally, we should have a ratio of omega-3 to omega-6 in our diets of 1:2, but because so few of us eat enough food sources of omega-3, the typical ratio in many Westernized diets is 1:10 or 1:20. Not only do we cook using more vegetable fat, but this is also an ingredient in the majority of processed foods – from biscuits to salad dressings – and is often in a positively unhealthy hydrogenated form to extend its shelf life.

Remember how your granny told you that fish was good for the brain? She was right. Omega-3 fatty acids, DHA (docosahexaenoic acid) and EPA (eicosapentaenoic acid) are only available from oily fish such as mackerel, herring, salmon (preferably wild ocean salmon rather than farmed) and tuna. Omega-3 fatty acids are available in vegetable sources such as flaxseeds (linseeds) and green vegetables, but in the form of ALA (alpha lipoic acid), which needs converting to EPA and DHA, and this is often hampered because the human body is not good at this conversion process. Some medical conditions, for example diabetes and some allergies, can interfere with this conversion process too. Many people who rely on vegetable sources of omega-3 EFAs may be getting very little, or negligible amounts, of the active ingredient. The only way to be sure of getting an adequate intake of omega-3s is by eating oily fish.

If you opt to take a fish oil supplement, of which there are masses to choose from, it's worth considering what you are spending your money on. DHA is critical for the formulation of the brain, while EPA is necessary for its functioning capacity. So, for adults and those wanting to improve their brain function, a supplement of omega-3 EPA is the one to choose. However, if you are pregnant and want to make sure your developing child is getting the DHA necessary, choose a supplement that also includes DHA. Also take a look at the dosage. A fish oil supplement that provides 1000mg of 'fish oil' may not provide very much active ingredient per capsule. You need to see what the breakdown of ingredients is, because you want to aim for a supplement of around 500mg of EPA a day to gain any sort of therapeutic effect. So, if the 1000mg of fish oil capsule is providing you with only 50mg of EPA per capsule, you would need to take 10 a day. This could, in turn, provide you with too much vitamin A, also a constituent of fish oil and toxic in large quantities, so look for a product that provides a purer form of EPA. This may be a more expensive option, but will probably work out as more effective, and cheaper, in the long run. Look for a product that provides around 200mg to 300mg of EPA per capsule, and take two a day. It may also include some DHA, which is fine, and vitamin E – which is an antioxidant and used as a natural preservative for the product.

Clinical research published in March 2008 by the *Australian and New Zealand Journal of Psychiatry* showed EPA to be as clinically effective for depression as Prozac. Given that depression reduces our ability to focus and concentrate, EPA will help towards improving this, as other studies (mainly with children showing signs of attention deficit) carried out by Professor Basant Puri and Dr Alex Richardson have also shown. It's not entirely clear yet why EPA is so beneficial to brain function, but it is thought to be partly to do with the fact that it increases cell membrane fluidity in the brain, which crucially affects the efficiency of cell connectivity, even acting as 'second messengers' for some neurotransmitters and, as a consequence, helping to improve brain function.

IRON

Iron is one supplement that is sometimes necessary when iron-deficiency anaemia has occurred. However, in the long term, it is better to improve dietary sources of iron than to supplement. Iron is an essential component of haemoglobin, which transports oxygen in the blood to all parts of the body. It also plays a vital role in many metabolic reactions. Iron deficiency can cause anaemia resulting from low levels of haemoglobin in the blood. Iron deficiency is the most widespread mineral nutritional deficiency both in Britain and worldwide, and up to 20 per cent of women in developed countries have iron-deficiency anaemia. Iron from animal sources, like meat, is more easily absorbed, but many vegetables and fruit provide good sources – spinach, chickpeas, broccoli, dried apricots, dried figs, baked beans, for example. Tannin in tea inhibits absorption, as does excessive fibre in the diet. Vitamin C greatly improves absorption, especially that from non-animal sources.

Substances that affect brain functioning

Suffice to say that it isn't just what we eat – or don't eat – that can affect how we function intellectually: there are many other substances that are ingested in different ways, often for recreational reasons, that have a dramatic effect on brain functioning and concentration. Some substances – caffeine and nicotine, for example – can have a stimulating effect, and are habitually used to promote intellectual performance in the short term. Others such as alcohol or cannabis we use to relax. However, understanding how these substances work, and how they may affect us in the long term, may be valuable in deciding whether their effect on our concentration, ability to focus and achieve is beneficial or otherwise.

CAFFEINE

Caffeine, or trimethylxathine, is probably the most widely used stimulant in the world, present in coffee and to some extent tea, and also in everyday caffeinated drinks such as cola (which contain between 10 to 50mg) and those designed to give an energy boost, such as Red Bull (as much as 80mg) per can. A typical cup of coffee contains around 100mg of caffeine, and a cup of tea around half as much. Once in the bloodstream, caffeine attaches itself to nerve cells, which fire up in readiness for an emergency – hence its highly stimulating effect. What this also does is stop another more calming and naturally occurring substance called adenosine from attaching to those same nerve cells. Adenosine works in our bodies to damp down nervous activity, calming cells and slowing things down. So not only does caffeine rev you up (and you can often notice your heart beating faster when you have a coffee) but it also stops the natural agents that would otherwise be keeping you (your nerve cells) calm.

Over time, and because of this reduced exposure to adenosine the nerve cells become supersensitive to its calming effect, and without the effect of caffeine, things automatically slow down, including our blood pressure, and we can feel lethargic and headachy – both common symptoms of caffeine withdrawal. Caffeine also increases levels of dopamine in the brain, contributing to its addictive effect (see below for more on dopamine). Although an excess of caffeine can have unwanted side effects – the overstimulation of nerve cells causes insomnia, irritability and heart palpitations – because the symptoms of withdrawal are also unpleasant, people find it difficult to give up.

The positive benefits of caffeine of making you feel alert, focused and better able to concentrate on a task for an extended period of time – which makes it the number-one 'free drug' companies hand out to employees they want to get the most out of – can be outweighed by its overuse, which can provoke the unwanted side effects listed above. Don't underestimate its negative side and use with care – and try to cut down altogether if you have any problems with insomnia.

NICOTINE

Nicotine is another sneaky, addictive chemical that fools the brain into thinking that the body needs to get active, by stimulating excitement hormones, and it can increase the jitters. When a cigarette is smoked, nicotine from the tobacco is inhaled and enters the bloodstream via the lungs. It fools the brain into thinking it's an action chemical, acetylcholine, which causes noradrenalin to be secreted. This 'fight or flight' hormone prepares the body for major activity, so, initially at least, everything gears up: heart rate and blood pressure rise, attention and memory improve, and appetite diminishes, stimulating the body. Nicotine also stimulates the release of dopamine – that feel-good hormone which is so addictive. Trouble is, in the long term cigarette smoking is detrimental to the health of the smoker, damaging the lungs and inhibiting oxygen intake to the body's cells, including the brain, eventually damaging intellectual function.

ALCOHOL

Alcohol is the most commonly available, socially acceptable intoxicant, which is, technically speaking, a nervous system depressant. The active ingredient of alcohol is ethanol, which is easily absorbed by the blood, and works by increasing the effectiveness of GABA, the neurotransmitter gamma-aminobutyrate. GABA's primary function is to calm the brain down, so it depresses its activity. Alcohol also stimulates the release of feel-good chemicals such as dopamine and endorphins, which, of course, encourage its continued use and can lead to alcohol-dependent behaviour. Ethanol, is, however, toxic to the body, so becoming physically addicted to a toxic substance will also cause long-term physical damage as all major organs, including the brain, become adversely affected.

In the short term, the effects of excessive alcohol consumption, and its resulting hangover, can affect the way we are able to focus and concentrate over the following twenty-four hours – as anyone who has tried to manage a full day's work with a hangover can testify. Regular excessive drinking, however, means not only regular hangovers and poor performance because of that, but that the accumulative and corrosive effects of a toxin on the brain eventually affect all the higher cognitive functions – memory, judgement, comprehension, decision making, planning, reasoning, etc. – and diminish intellectual ability as a consequence. A physical addiction to alcohol means that without it, withdrawal symptoms of being physically jittery, sweaty and shaky occur, alleviated only by more alcohol. Recovery from physical dependency takes time and usually means complete abstinence from alcohol in the future to prevent a relapse, and a degree of damage to the body may be irreversible. In young people, where the brain has greater plasticity, the damage can be greater and for this reason teenage binge-drinking should be a serious concern.

CANNABIS

Many people will tell you that alcohol is a more dangerous recreational drug than cannabis, and in some ways that is true. Alcohol is more prevalent and socially acceptable, it is legal and it is the biggest cause of drug-related violence and accidents from street brawls to car crashes, while cannabis makes users relaxed and, well, dopey. It is, however, a potent and commonly available drug and the concern in recent years is about a variety that is particularly potent, commonly known as skunk, and what long-term effect this may have on users, especially those who have started using it in adolescence.

The chemical in cannabis responsible for its effect on the body and brain is THC – tetrahydrocannabinol. THC binds to a specific protein receptor, the cannabinoid receptor CB1 that occurs throughout the central nervous system, so it affects the function of the whole central nervous system – and its short-term effects include changes in perception, lowered blood pressure, impairment of coordination, concentration and short-term memory. THC remains easily detectable in the body for several days, and some more sensitive tests can show evidence of it some weeks later. It finds its way into the hippocampus, where memory pathways are formed; into the cortex, responsible for reasoning and other important cognitive skills; into the hypothalamus, which controls our most primitive urges like hunger (hence the munchies associated with cannabis use); and also into the cerebellum, where movement and coordination are controlled. Cannabis makes the user less focused, motivated and willing to perform – it provokes a sense of relaxation and laissez-faire. It can be used to positive effect as a painkiller for those with cancer, arthritis and multiple sclerosis, but in the UK it remains a Class B drug, so even though widely used – mostly for recreational rather than medicinal use – it is illegal.

One emerging concern is over the use of cannabis among young people, whose developing brains seem to be more vulnerable to the effects of using it. Research published by the Institute of Psychiatry in London found that up to 25 per cent of those who started smoking cannabis as teenagers were found to be five times more likely to develop psychotic illnesses like schizophrenia. It appears that there may be a gene variant in some people that makes their still-developing brain more susceptible to the impact of cannabis on their dopamine levels and that this, along with the impact of THC, may be relevant to the development of the disease.

Increasingly prevalent, skunk is considered to be up to ten times more potent than resin or grass, and it is this form of cannabis that is causing most concern. In 2006 in the UK, more than 22,000 people were treated by the NHS for addiction and psychological problems associated with smoking skunk. In 2007, Antonio Maria Costa, the executive director of the United Nations Office on Drugs and Crime, said: 'The cannabis now in circulation is many times more powerful than the weed which today's ageing baby-boomers smoked in college. Evidence of the damage to mental health caused by cannabis use – from loss of concentration to paranoia, aggressiveness and outright psychosis – is mounting and cannot be ignored.'

COCAINE

Cocaine was once hailed as a miracle cure, for everything from toothache to depression – in fact, in the 1880s, Sigmund Freud was among the many practitioners who regularly prescribed it. It is derived from the coca plant in South America, where the native population enjoyed – and probably still do – chewing the leaves, which release miniscule amounts of cocaine, for thousands of years. Cocaine prevents inhibition of the release of noradrenalin, serotonin and dopamine in the brain. The user is suddenly exposed to huge quantities of feel-good hormones and stimulants, making them feel euphoric, acutely able and social.

However, the risk of having a heart attack within an hour of use is increased by twenty-four times. Coming down after such an experience creates a dramatically contrasting low mood and, because of its addictive nature, repeated use becomes the norm. In the longer term, the effects are literally mind-altering and both paranoid delusions and hallucinations can occur.

Are you stressed?

It's not just external influences like caffeine or cannabis that can disturb our equilibrium. We are quite capable of creating our own internal disturbances through persistent negative thoughts and even worrying which, if taken to extreme, can distract and disturb us. The mind is a powerful tool that can exert considerable influence over our behaviour. It is well known that negative thoughts and anxiety can stop us functioning to the best of our ability, both mentally and physically. So too can stress. Stress is so common it is now considered a normal part of everyday life. But as a response, stress was only ever designed to be intermittent, gearing us up mentally and physically to achieve something in the short term, not for it to become a way of life. It is one of those states of being that can creep up on you, so insidiously that it can become almost overwhelming before being recognized. Far better then to be aware, and to keep a check on it before it becomes a problem. Use stress effectively in the short term, to gear you up to deliver that presentation, for example, but don't let it become a way of life, or something you deal with by using more caffeine, more alcohol or more carbohydrates to get you through.

Anxiety

Global connectivity has led to global worries on an unprecedented scale. One country's credit crunch is no longer an isolated experience, it affects us all, and even if it doesn't affect us immediately, we live in fear that sometime soon it might. A survey carried out in August 2008 by the UK's Mental Health Foundation found very real worries existing as a consequence. The survey revealed that 80 per cent of British adults were worried about the impact of the current financial climate on their finances, and 61 per cent said that money worries are always at the back of their mind. Almost twice as many people aged 18 to 24 were stressed by financial woes as those aged 55-plus (40 per cent in comparison to 22 per cent). And there were gender differences – 1 in 4 men (23 per cent) said they have no money anxieties at all, in comparison to only 1 in 10 women (13 per cent). Rising fuel (76 per cent) and food (70 per cent) prices were people's biggest economic worries; 20 per cent were concerned about their mortgage repayments – the same number as those worried about not being able to buy clothes, shoes and gadgets – while 1 in 3 were apprehensive about repaying credit cards, loans and other debts.

Increased communication, with bad news being relayed around the world in seconds, means that we are alert to catastrophes as they happen. Even though the threat of terrorism is, statistically, unlikely to actually affect us personally, worrying about it is pervasive. Will climate change end life as we know it? No one can yet answer that, but it won't stop us from worrying.

Anxiety is a normal and helpful state if you are confronted by a challenging or potential dangerous situation, when it is part of the 'fight or flight' (or freeze) response, which produces a surge of adrenalin and other stress hormones into the bloodstream. It is the imagined or perceived threat of something that makes us feel anxious, which in turn creates the physical symptoms of anxiety, which can include jitteriness, tension, increased heart rate, difficulty breathing and sweaty palms. When this becomes a persistent state of being, then it's extremely unhelpful. Whether you are anxious about the risk to your job or your elderly parent's health, anxiety can become an all-pervasive backdrop to your life when it becomes impossible to let it go and shift your thoughts to other, more productive, areas. Because of the

◈ FOCUSING EXERCISE – TAKE FIVE

When you feel as if stress is mounting, threatening to overwhelm you and certainly inhibiting your concentration, then 'take five'. Take five minutes to do a simple focusing exercise to gather your thoughts, eliminate the negative gremlins that have begun to circulate and refresh your mind.

Start by closing your eyes and deliberately relaxing your shoulders. Breathe in to a count of five, pause for a count of five, and then breathe out gently to a count of five. Continue with this pattern. Once your breath has steadied, and you can feel your muscles releasing tension, start counting back from one hundred in fives: 100, 95, 90, 85, 80, etc. Focus on the numbers as you count, emptying your mind of all other thoughts. When you have reached zero, pause again and focus on your breathing. Open your eyes, and resume whatever activity you had paused.

possible protective function of anxiety, the primitive part of our brain, the limbic system, is more easily hard wired for anxiety than it is for positive optimism – that is, feeling anxious can become almost like a habit. Constantly worrying about life begins to feel 'normal' and many people begin to experience what the medics have come to call a 'generalized anxiety disorder'.

This type of anxiety is characterized by excessively worrying about everything, even small inconsequential things, most of the time, for a period of at least six months or more. These feelings of anxiety, and the associated physical symptoms that occur, interfere significantly with the ability to function socially, at work or in relationships. As well as worrying, the physical impact creates feelings of restlessness or being constantly on edge or irrationally irritable, feeling very tired and lethargic, muscular tension, headaches, insomnia and an inability to sleep well. The consequences of feeling like this are considerable. It takes up a lot of time and energy, and is counterproductive to being able to focus and concentrate. It can also lead to burnout or depression.

Burnout and adrenal exhaustion

Do you feel exhausted, wrung out, trapped, angry or dissociated? Are you working harder and longer but achieving less? Do you constantly feel under the weather, or suffer from constant aches, pains, niggles and minor illnesses that won't go away? Dr Dina Glouberman, psychotherapist and author of *The Joy of Burnout*, describes the classic signs of burnout as:

O a growing emotional, mental and/or physical exhaustion that isn't alleviated by sleeping
O an increasing sense of being cut off from ourselves and other people
O a decreasing ability to be effective at doing what we have always done, at work or at home.

Remember, burnout isn't just an emotional state: there's also a physical impact. Constantly living on edge, and failing to get adequate nutrition, rest and relaxation, means that in times of stress, the nervous system responds by churning out lots more hormones – adrenalin, noradrenalin and cortisol – designed to keep you going in the short term while you are short on sleep, regular food and time to rest. It's that old 'fight or flight' reaction again and what's crucial about this is that it's designed for the *short term*. Maintaining this state is not good for the body. The adrenal glands which produce these hormones become overstimulated and can become damaged so that, over time, they become unpredictable – sometimes failing to produce enough hormones on demand, sometimes overproducing – leaving you feeling alternatively completed floored and depleted or wired and panicky. Ultimately, the adrenals can virtually pack up, creating the risk of Chronic Fatigue Syndrome, ME (mylagic encephalitis), fibromyalgia and other autoimmune disorders like lupus and rheumatoid arthritis. Complete burnout is really the final stage of adrenal exhaustion.

Not monitoring your stress levels and your health can mean that early signs of burnout may lead to adrenal exhaustion – and the first sign may be a shift in our ability to concentrate.

Symptoms of adrenal exhaustion include:

O difficulties with concentration and memory
O insomnia
O low-stress tolerance, irritability
O lethargy and fatigue
O light-headedness when standing up
O allergies
O PMS (premenstrual syndrome)
O more frequent coughs and colds.

Of course you can get some or all of these symptoms, to a greater or lesser degree, for other reasons. But if you know you are pushing yourself and you have several long-standing but minor health problems that might be related to your lifestyle, reassess what you can do to avoid them escalating into a major problem with long-term consequences.

Are you getting enough sleep?

Sleep is essential to restore the body and mind. Deep slow-wave sleep, when our brain moves into delta waves, is imperative: this is the proper, restorative sleep that will restore you physically as well as mentally. Without adequate sleep, not only do we feel tired and irritable and unable to focus and concentrate, but we also suffer a form of physical stress, so we produce more stress hormones (adrenalin and cortisol) to compensate, making us even less likely to sleep. This form of stress is also inflammatory

– hence the secretion of anti-inflammation hormones like cortisol – and damages the cells of the body, causing permanent long-term damage over time. This is also why many think that some people respond to chronic stress by developing serious illnesses like cancer, heart disease, diabetes and arthritis. Constantly circulating cortisol, which in persistently high levels is a neurotoxin, will also damage the brain. Stress hormones are designed for short, sharp restorative action, not for sustaining you against chronic levels of perpetual stress caused by your lifestyle.

Add to this our tendency to resort to artificial stimulants like caffeine, nicotine and alcohol to keep us going and there's another problem. High intakes of these artificial stimulants will wake us up in the short term, but make it even more difficult to sleep well in the long. It's a vicious circle.

In 2008, the online health site NetDoctor carried out a survey after noticing a surge in hits to its website from users looking for advice on insomnia. The results showed that nearly half of the 1,000 men and women who answered the online questionnaire said they were sleeping less well now than they were a year ago. Twenty per cent said that they were regularly getting less than five hours' sleep a night, while 25 per cent woke up more than three times a night. Ten per cent said it took two hours or more for them to get to sleep each night, and of those who woke during the night, 63 per cent found it hard to get back to sleep. Stress was cited as a major factor, with two-thirds blaming money and work worries for their insomnia. Half of those who responded said they would like to sleep longer than eight hours per night, if they could, yet less than a fifth (17 per cent) said they were able to.

Sleeping better and increasing the amount of sleep you have are easily improved. If you feel as if you have constant jet lag, and getting up in the morning is always tricky, it might be time to reset your internal clock by going to bed regularly at a reasonable hour, and setting the alarm to get up at a consistent hour, eight hours later. It can take several days to reset your internal clock, but you can only benefit.

Poor posture

It may not be immediately obvious how poor posture could have an impact on concentration, but it is worth considering for a moment how a sedentary life, for example, and sitting for long periods of time, can affect posture and how this, in turn, might affect concentration. Bad posture can cause poor breathing patterns, restricted circulation, muscular strain and repetitive strain injuries, which can not only sap energy but also cause constant, low-grade physical pain. This may be only a niggle that, eventually, increases the risk of headaches, or it could be a debilitating back problem. Or it could affect your ability to sleep well at night. Trying to concentrate under these circumstances becomes difficult and, if poor posture is to blame, then it's worth taking steps to rectify it.

Ways to improve posture include making sure you sit well when working at a desk, making sure your chair is at the correct height and sitting on an exercise ball, which prevents you slouching. Regular stretching exercises that will alleviate the tension in muscles that are held in limited positions for long periods of time will also help, as will taking up regular yoga or swimming, or Pilates – which also has the benefit of strengthening your core muscles, thus improving your posture further. Freeing up your posture, alleviating the tension in your many muscle groups from shoulders to calves, will also enhance the circulation of the blood around the body – and, because the blood carries oxygen, this should also help you feel less tired.

Conclusion

○ **What you eat will determine how well you are concentrating.** And it's not just a grumbling stomach that can distract you from a particular task. Low or see-sawing blood-sugar levels will have a direct effect not just on energy levels but also on mood and the ability to concentrate. The brain needs adequate fuel to function and poor nutrition will lead to poor performance and poor concentration. Fact.

○ **Coffee can help you concentrate better – but only in the short term,** and if you rely on it, instead of learning the art of concentration, you may end up being able to concentrate less well. Most of the time. Caffeine also stops the body's own naturally calming agents from doing their job, so you may find, if you depend on coffee, that you end up more distracted and stressed and less able to concentrate for longer periods of time.

○ **Anxiety is the number-one mental health problem in the UK.** And since the collapse of the global financial markets, worrying about money now tops the list of problems that can exacerbate feelings of stress. These in turn make concentration more difficult. Relaxation techniques and physical exercise can help stop anxiety turning into chronic stress and actually work to boost powers of concentration.

○ **Drink alcohol in moderation.** If you've ever suffered a hangover, then you'll already know how hard it is to focus and concentrate with one – you just want the day to end. Worse than that, excessive drinking is actually toxic to the brain and will affect all the higher functions, including memory, judgement, planning, reasoning and comprehension, making concentrating in any meaningful way impossible.

○ **If you want to concentrate better, get a good night's sleep.** The brain switches to its delta-wave patterns during deep, slow-wave sleep, which is crucial for restoring the body and the mind. Sleep deprivation not only leaves you feeling tired, irritable and unable to concentrate properly, but also triggers the release of stress hormones which, in excess, can then make it difficult to get a good night's sleep. Break this cycle before it damages your health, as well as your ability to concentrate.

CHAPTER THREE
What else is stopping you?

You can always find a distraction
if you're looking for one.
Tom Kite, US golf professional

If only they would stop doing the
wrong, the right will do itself.
F.M. Alexander

You may have become used to the level at which you concentrate. You may think it is adequate. You may think
that you don't need to concentrate any more than you
already do. But you may also have a sneaking suspicion that if
you could concentrate better, you might be a whole lot more
successful at what you want to do – whether you want to
pass an exam, learn a new skill or just get things done more
efficiently; and not only that, but once you improve your concentration skills, then you'd have more time to do what you
really want to concentrate on.

We have no difficulty concentrating on what we like to do,
but getting things done that we have less interest in is another
matter. Your teenage son preferring his PS3 to his geography

homework is a case in point. Or you may find that you have put off that report that needs writing for weeks, even when you know from experience that once you get started, it won't actually take that much time to complete. In fact, you have spent almost more time thinking about it, picking it up and putting it down, starting and stopping, cleaning the kitchen, walking the dog, phoning a friend than it would actually take to write it. Why? Because you don't find the idea of it very interesting.

We are all expert at finding ways to sabotage our attempts to concentrate. We become easy to distract, we procrastinate, we daydream, we multitask – all of which stop us concentrating fully. Trouble is, the longer we do this, the easier it is to become used to this way of doing it. Working in this distracted, half-hearted, time-consuming way begins to feel normal. To stop doing this takes time and discipline, as learning any new habit does, and we have to be alert to what it is that we do that stops us concentrating, and understand why it's so counterproductive.

It was Linda Stone, who previously worked at Apple and Microsoft and is now a writer and consultant, who first coined the phrase 'continual partial attention'. She believes that over the past twenty years we have become experts at this way of working. She says:

> We have pushed ourselves to an extreme. Continuous partial attention is an 'always on, anywhere, anytime, any-place behaviour' that creates an artificial sense of crisis. We are always on high alert, scanning the periphery to see if we are missing other opportunities. If we are, our fickle attention shifts focus. What's ringing? Who is it? How many emails? What's on my list? What time is it in Beijing? In this state of always-on crisis, our highly charged, adrenalin-fuelled 'fight or flight' mechanism kicks in. This is great when we are being chased by tigers, but how many of those 500 emails a day is a tiger? Is everything really an emergency? The way we currently use technologies would have us believe it is.

This comes from a desire not to miss out, speculates Stone. But, she cautions, there is a downside. 'Many of us feel the "shadow side" of CPA – overstimulation and lack of fulfillment. The latest, greatest technologies are now contributing to our feeling of being increasingly powerless. Researchers are beginning to tell us that we may actually be doing tasks more slowly and poorly.'

Distraction

There are two main types of distraction – internal and external. Internal distractions include the voice in your head (that constant, sniping, irritating, internal critic) and daydreaming, while external distractions include the telephone ringing, noises in the street, other people. There's no doubt that some people are more easily distractible than others, but it is also possible to learn how to filter out distraction – which is very worthwhile, because research has shown that those who are more easily distracted produce worse test results. Dutch social psychologist and researcher Harm Veling, from the Department of Psychology at the University of Nijmegen in the Netherlands, has proved that the brain selects incoming information to remember useful things, while distracting information is inhibited. The test he designed revealed that the participants remembered distracting information less well than relevant or neutral information. In addition, those people who were better at excluding the deliberately distracting information performed the task quicker. But the ability to ignore, or suppress, distractions is conscious and not automatic: when participants were tired they were more susceptible to distraction and performed less well.

It seems, too, that there are two distinct parts of the brain that operate when it comes to concentration and distraction, according to research carried out at MIT in the US and published in 2007. Scientists previously knew that paying attention involved multiple brain regions, but they didn't know how because they had studied only one area of the brain at a time. This new research, led by neuroscientist Earl Miller, involved looking at how two areas of the brain reacted together when the subject was made to jump to attention.

In Miller's experiment, monkeys were trained to take attention tests on a video screen in return for a reward of apple juice. They had to concentrate on picking out and matching coloured shapes that appeared on the screen, while every now and then another brightly coloured shape would flash up, serving as a distraction. When the monkeys were deliberately concentrating on the task, the prefrontal cortex – the executive centre at the front of the brain – was activated. But when something distracting grabbed the monkeys' attention, the parietal cortex, towards the back of the brain, revved up.

The electrical activity in these two areas began vibrating in synchrony as they signalled each other, but they vibrated at different frequencies, almost as if they were at different places on a radio dial. This showed that sustaining concentration involved lower-frequency neuron activity, while distraction occurred at higher frequencies. Miller concluded that maybe, one day, it would be possible to identify a way to influence the ability to boost concentration by somehow counteracting the higher-frequency neuron activity stimulated by distraction.

The interaction of these two, physically distinct, parts of the brain has caught the attention of scientists at the forefront of brain function and performance research. It makes sense that there should be two ways in which attention works: the sort of reflex attention when something might be a threat, which is a useful survival tool, and the kind of deliberate attention that makes concentration possible, which is more of a learned application. Identifying the two ways in which the brain pays attention may help us understand better what can get in the way of voluntary attention (the ability to concentrate). Scientists already know from studies on attention deficit disorders that some people have trouble filtering out distractions, while others have difficulty focusing. It might eventually become pos-

STOP! METHOD TO AVOID DISTRACTING THOUGHTS

As part of the process of learning to be completely focused, you may have to practise the Stop! method. This is a very simple way of consciously noticing when your attention has wandered and saying Stop! to yourself. Rather than consciously trying not to think about anything else, focus on what you need to focus on, but whenever a stray thought encroaches on it, say Stop! which will, in time, work to bring your attention back quickly. You will probably have to do this over and over again at first. Keep at it, because eventually (even if this takes a number of weeks of practice) you will find that you are saying Stop! to yourself much less frequently as your ability to concentrate improves.

Some people even wear a rubber band around their wrist, and instead of saying Stop! they ping it against their wrist when they sense their thoughts beginning to distract them. The sharp ping is mildly painful, and instantly stops the thought and refocuses the mind.

sible to override what might be either an innate or a learned tendency for the brain's parietal cortex to react to stimuli in an unhelpful way.

Daydreaming

There is some argument supporting the notion that a certain amount of daydreaming can be both creative and constructive. Idly thinking through ideas can lead to some interesting breakthroughs, as many from scientists to entrepreneurs have found over the years with their 'Eureka!' moments; but in a culture that values ostentatious productivity, daydreaming can look like doing nothing. And in some cases it is. Described as a visual exercise in escapism, it can be just a pleasurable way to pass the time and, in some mundane tasks, it can help relieve boredom. However, some daydreaming can achieve an almost meditative state and relies on a degree of concentration to achieve it – so how can you identify positive daydreaming? And, in terms of some downtime for your brain, could daydreaming be a positive habit to cultivate?

Mainstream psychology research hasn't yet paid much attention to daydreaming, but more recently a spate of new studies has been chipping away at its mysteries and scientists say the topic is beginning to gain visibility. In 2007, Professor Michael Kane, a psychologist at the University of North Carolina at Greensboro in the US, published the results of some research where college students were tested for the amount of time they daydreamed. He sampled the thoughts of students at eight random times a day for a week, and found that on average, they were not thinking about what they were doing 30 per cent of the time. For some students it was between 80 and 90 per cent of the time, with only one student of the 126 participants denying any mind-wandering at the sampled moments.

Future research may reveal ways to reap pay-offs from the habit, and show ways to help students keep their focus on their studies, and car drivers to keep their minds on the road. And it may shed more light on Attention Deficit Hyperactivity Disorder (ADHD), which can include an unusually severe inability to focus, which causes trouble in multiple areas of life. More generally, daydreaming is worth studying because it's just too common to ignore, and this suggests that it may have a value or some aspect that can be harnessed. In fact, because daydreaming links together series of nice thoughts, ideas and images in a pleasurable way, it requires a certain amount of concentration to be able to do it. If you are unable to control and order your thoughts in any sort of logical or sequential way, they remain completely random. Some children with attention deficit disorders, who have never learned to control their attention, find daydreaming impossible: their inability to focus inhibits their ability to do even this, which means they don't have access to this important intellectual resource. But while daydreaming shows some evidence that you can concentrate – which can be built on – it also requires you to develop a more mindful discipline to 'park' those thoughts when they are impeding concentration, so that they don't intrude inappropriately.

Procrastination

'Procrastination is the thief of time' – how many times have you heard that? And it's true. How many times have you found yourself phoning a friend rather than starting a piece of work you don't want to do; or vacuuming the sitting-room floor rather than doing your tax return? How many times have you had a two-week deadline and waited until the last minute? There's always a good reason not to do something you don't want to do, and experts have worked out the main reasons we procrastinate:

O poor time-management
O difficulty concentrating
O fear and anxiety about the task at hand
O negative beliefs that you won't succeed
O personal problems, ranging from finances to your love life
O finding the task boring
O unrealistic expectations and the quest for perfection
O fear of failure.

In the twenty-first century, we've created the perfect environment for procrastination with the many distractions we allow ourselves, from TV to the internet, mobile phones to email: we never switch off. We may also have become highly adept at looking really busy, tackling all these seemingly 'urgent' tasks when really we're just procrastinating. Is it any wonder we never get anything done?

Procrastination is characterized by a deferment of actions or tasks until a later time, and psychology researchers have cited three behavioural criteria to categorize it: that which is counterproductive, needless or delaying. Anything unrelated to the job that needs doing serves as procrastination. So, if you have a report to write and you defer it to play solitaire on the laptop, then that's procrastination. Loss of productivity is a direct result of procrastination.

Some people will use procrastination to deliberately create a crisis – when you leave something to the last minute, it becomes critical and stress levels rise as you attempt to complete the task – because they feel more able to deliver under these circumstances. Personality types commonly referred to as 'drama queens' use this tactic to motivate themselves.

Research on the physical causes of procrastination has looked at the role of the prefrontal cortex, the area of the brain involved in executive functions like planning, impulse control and focusing attention, and which also acts as a filter to distracting stimuli. If this area of the brain is functioning under par, for some reason, procrastination may be a symptom. In the developing brain, and especially in adolescence when this area of the brain is underdeveloped, procrastination can cause major problems with schoolwork and, later, the work of students at college – hence the traditional picture of late-night epic writing efforts and, when these fail, missed essay deadlines.

It also takes energy to procrastinate, valuable energy that is more or less wasted, and that you could be using on concentrating. As an activity, procrastination dissipates energy and distracts you, even protecting you against risking the anxiety or concern that may be an integral part of doing what you should be doing.

Procrastination can, however, become a bad habit, leading to stress, anxiety, chronic underperformance and loss of confidence, all of which will erode your ability to concentrate.

✦ MAKING LISTS

Making a 'to do' list can be a helpful way of committing specific tasks to paper to avoid forgetting them, rather than constantly trying to keep them in mind, which can be distracting. But making lists requires some discipline; otherwise it can become just another form of procrastination. So, start each day with five minutes' planning, and make a list that prioritizes what needs doing first and includes only those things that must be done that day, and work your way through it. The list can include doing a particular task that requires concentration, but also a note of a phone call that needs making, or a bill that needs paying, so that you can concentrate rather than have this nagging concern at the back of your mind. But be realistic about what you can achieve in any one day – you can always add things to the list later – and as you work your way through give your undivided attention to each task, which will also help you execute the task more efficiently.

Whether lack of concentration is a cause of procrastination, or procrastination is leading to a failure to concentrate properly, it can become a vicious cycle, so it's worth addressing and breaking the cycle, especially as persistent procrastination reinforces all the negative feelings that made it such an attractive alternative in the first place.

Piers Steel, professor of business studies at the University of Calgary in Canada, has made procrastination the focus of a three-year study. Fortunately he's also identified some pointers to help us (and, if you feel like procrastinating right now, you will find a tool to measure your level of procrastination on his website, www.procrastinus.com).

Autopilot

A lot of what we do every day we can do on autopilot. In fact, autopilot is a useful way of accomplishing some tasks, like the washing up, that do not require high levels of concentration. But sometimes, doing a task on autopilot can be counterproductive to actually learning or retaining information. How many times have you read a book only to realize, as you get to the end of the page, that you can't remember a word you've read? You have, as it were, been going through the motions, while thinking about something completely different, and as a result, you haven't retained any of the information you've just read. Whether you were distracted by your own internal thoughts, the noise from the street or the music on the radio, you have been on autopilot while you were reading, and so have achieved nothing. This is more likely to happen with a subject in which you have limited interest, even if it's important you get to grips with the information for, say, work or an exam.

If you find this is the case, you need to look at ways to increase your concentration while you read – maybe by taking notes, or even reading out loud; otherwise, you're just wasting your time. Functioning on autopilot can happen in other situations, including social events, and can be unhelpful. It can also be exacerbated by tiredness, when it can be downright dangerous, for example when driving a car.

Multitasking

So you think you're really good at multitasking, and that you can concentrate just as well doing more than one thing at a time? Think again. You may be giving the impression you are doing a lot, but the reality is often something different. Now that we have access to functional MRI scans, which can actually see, monitor and record what our brains are doing while we're doing it, scientists know a lot more, and what we now know is that multitasking could mean that you are doing nothing well enough to gain any benefits.

In an experiment carried out at the University of California, Los Angeles, a group of 20-something students were asked to sort through index cards in two trials. The first time, the students worked in silence and during the second exact-same task they were asked to listen out for specific tones in a series of randomly presented sounds. The way their brains coped with this was to transfer from the hippocampus, the part of the brain that stores and recalls information, to the striatum, which handles repetitive activities. They had no trouble doing the same task while distracted, but they found it much more difficult afterwards to remember what, exactly, they had been sorting. So their ability to do the task in a way that meant they later remembered it was compromised, which tells us that if you are trying to learn a new skill, you won't do it as well or as easily if you are distracted while you are doing it.

The neuroplasticity of our brains means that they are built to manage a variety of tasks at once, but only up to a point. It seems that this physiological balancing act we ask of our brains comes at a cost. By constantly switching back and forth between tasks, and by stimulating parts of the brain that are concerned with visual processing and physical coordination, as in the experiment described above, we appear to distract from the higher areas of the brain related to memory and learning. We can end up concentrating on the process of concentrating, rather than on what we were supposed to be concentrating on. Much of the time it probably won't matter much, but it's easy to see how inefficient multitasking is if you are trying to learn something. Concentrate well and do it once; distract yourself and you may have to do something several times before it's learned. And when it comes to storing information that you want to recall later, perhaps when revising for an exam, you won't learn it so well if you don't concentrate while you're learning. Focusing or concentrating well means that you store information in the part of the brain necessary for later recall.

True, there are some forms of multitasking that do work, but this usually involves only doing a maximum of two things at once, one of which is done automatically – for example, washing up and listening to the radio. Washing up doesn't really take much thought, so 95 per cent of your concentration can be given over to the other task in hand. This wouldn't apply to doing three tasks, though: washing up, listening to the radio and reading a book. It's just not possible to absorb either the book or the radio adequately, so – along with the practical difficulties of doing all three at once – you probably wouldn't bother. However, there are some activities that appear automatic but actually require good concentration to be effective, as the ban on driving while simultaneously using your mobile phone now recognizes. Driving may appear to be an automatic skill but it is a complex activity, requiring excellent concentration and good reaction times, both of which will be impaired if the driver is focusing on something else. Many experts also believe that talking on a hands-free phone is also too distracting to be entirely safe. 'Multitasking is always going to slow you down, increasing the chances of mistakes', says David Meyer, a cognitive scientist and Director of the Brain, Cognition and Action Laboratory at the University of Michigan in the US. 'Disruptions and interruptions are a bad deal from the standpoint of our ability to process information.'

Research carried out in 2007 at the Institute for the Future of the Mind at Oxford University would seem to reinforce this view. A study involved one group of 18-to 21-year-olds and a second group of 35-to 39-year-olds, who were given 90 seconds to translate images into numbers, using a simple code. The younger group did 10 per cent better when not interrupted, but when both groups were interrupted by a phone call, a text message or instant messaging, the older group matched the younger group in speed and accuracy. 'The older people think more slowly, but they have a faster fluid intelligence, so they are better able to block out interruptions and choose what to focus on', said Martin Westwell, deputy director of the institute, who admits that he has modified his work habits since completing the research project. 'I check my email much less often – the interruptions really can throw you off track.'

It is impossible to measure precisely lost productivity caused by multitasking, but in 2007, Jonathan Spira, chief analyst at Basex, a business research firm, estimated the cost of interruptions to the US economy at nearly $650 billion a year. This figure was based on surveys and interviews with professionals and office workers, which concluded that 28 per cent of their time was spent on what they considered to be interruptions (and recovery time) before they returned to their main tasks. Spira conceded that $650 billion is a rough estimate, and work interruptions will never, and should not be eliminated, because this is often how work is done and ideas are shared. But even if half of all those constant interruptions at work are worthwhile, the rest still represent a lot of money lost.

There may also be another cost to distraction resulting from multitasking. The process of constantly switching, multitasking, call it what you will, carries with it a degree of stress. Not necessarily one that you would even notice, but one that requires the key stress hormones (cortisol and adrenalin) to be secreted at higher levels to help you stay on top of what you are trying to do. These are the same hormones that are secreted when we need short, rapid bursts of energy necessary for 'fight or flight', but they are not designed for long-term use. In the short term, feeling constantly 'hyped' by high levels of stress hormones can result in the persistent 'brain fog' many of us experience, and in the long term, bombarding the brain with stress hormones that are neuro-toxic when secreted in large quantities may cause premature ageing and other brain damage. Interestingly, cortisol is what is known as a universal donor, which means it can attach to any receptor site and block the feel-good hormones, dopamine and serotonin, which help us feel calm and happy. So when we multitask not only are we stressed, but we are also missing out on the more positive effects of the body's own, natural antidotes. Hyper-vigilant, over-alert and anxious, it's hardly surprising we feel too stressed to concentrate.

Negative thinking

Our brains are automatically programmed for negative thinking; it is, if you like, our brain's default mode, born of a primal need to identify the negative and protect ourselves from it. This is, of course, all well and good when you have to be wary of an attack by marauding sabre-toothed tigers, but less useful when you are simply trying to get a piece of work done at your desk in the safety of your own home. You know the scenario: you sit down and pick up your book to read up on that new contractual information you need to know when pop! – that nasty little thought that says, You can't do this, it's too hard. Or, What makes you think you've got what it takes? Or, Did you see the way they looked at you when you arrived yesterday? Suddenly you go into a spiral of negative thought processes that are every bit as distracting as the music coming from your teenager's iPod headphones. The good news about negative thinking is that it's a habit that can be changed, but it's useful to first identify the common themes that may come up and sabotage your attempts to concentrate.

The idea that you can 'unlearn' self-defeating ways of thinking is the basis of cognitive, or 'thinking', therapies. In his book *Feeling Good: The New Mood Therapy*, psychiatrist Dr David Burns, an adjunct clinical professor of psychiatry and behavioural sciences at the Stanford University School of Medicine in the US, outlines a set of cognitive therapy techniques that people can use at home and at work, to help boost their self-confidence and break the cycle of repeated negative thinking. But before you can control destructive thoughts, you have to be able to recognize them, and Burns identifies what he and other cognitive behavioural therapists view as the major cognitive distortions that can open the door to a flood of unhelpful negative thinking.

○ **All-or-nothing thinking.** In this type of thinking, you're either a hero or a failure. Any small mistake marks you out as a complete failure. This kind of thinking can lead to crippling perfectionism.

○ **Overgeneralization.** Whenever something bad happens, you simply assume it's bound to happen again and again, rather than treating it as a one-off that you can learn from and thus avoid repeating.

○ **The mental filter.** You automatically dwell on the downside of any situation, while overlooking anything positive. So, instead of congratulating yourself on writing a great report, all you can see is the glaring typo on page 11 that it is too late to correct because you've sent it to your boss.

○ **Diminishing the positive.** In this kind of thinking, you tend to twist positive events into negative ones. If you just got a pay rise, for example, you may put yourself down for not getting a bigger one.

○ **Jumping to conclusions.** You become either a mind reader or a fortune teller – whatever it takes to see imagined trouble on the horizon.

○ **The binocular trick.** It's as if you're wearing magic lenses that only let you see everything blown out of proportion. Little problems become monstrous; major victories, trifling.

○ **Emotional reasoning.** You believe that your mood is a reflection of your true identity – you feel stupid, so you must be stupid – rather than understanding that maybe, on this occasion, you don't have all the tools or skills that you need to accomplish something.

○ **'Should' and 'must' thoughts.** You constantly remind yourself of things you should or must do. (One expert calls this 'musterbation'.) This can be completely counterproductive, especially when you constantly tell yourself that you must get something done or you should be able to concentrate.

○ **Labelling and mislabelling.** You tend to equate your 'self' with what you do, and since everyone makes mistakes, over time you develop a negative self-image based on errors you've made. So if you can't concentrate, it must be because you're stupid . . .

○ **Personalization.** You assume responsibility for anything that goes wrong, even when it's not your fault. Dr Burns calls this line of thinking 'the mother of guilt'.

With all this going on, is it any wonder you can't concentrate?

How your mood affects your ability to concentrate

Which came first: how you feel or the mood you're in? Does how you feel affect your mood or does your mood affect how you feel? Either way, there's no doubt that your mood can affect your ability to concentrate. If you are feeling calm and happy, then it's infinitely easier to concentrate than if you are feeling stressed or irritable. While stressed and irritable moods will distract you, calm and happy moods tend to encourage concentration. 'Moods are an internal measure of how we are,' says Dr Liz Miller, author of *Mood Mapping*. 'We do not express our moods directly. Instead, we express them indirectly in the way we think, communicate, behave and see the world. To concentrate, you need to feel good as well as having enough energy. Although concentration might look relaxed on the outside, it is work. And if you are concentrating intensely, it is hard work! You need to have enough energy to concentrate, and it is easier if you are also feeling positive.' But can you consciously change your mood? Yes, she says.

Miller devised the technique of Mood Mapping to enable her patients to understand what it was that might be influencing their moods, and what action they could take to improve their mood:

> Moods can be managed, both in the immediate moment and in the longer term. And to begin with you need to understand five key inputs to mood, which are: your surroundings, your physical body, your relationships, your knowledge and your nature (your personality type). Mood Mapping is a new technique that helps you first plot your mood and then work on it to get it right. It's a practical device that lets you see where your mood is coming from and enables you to identify those steps you need to take to manage it and stop it ruling your life.

Mood Mapping sees mood as having two parts: A, whether your energy level is high or low, and B, whether you are feeling positive or negative (good or bad). Combining these on the Mood Map (see opposite) gives four types of mood result:

1. **High energy, feeling positive**
   Result: action, motivated, achievement-oriented
2. **High energy, feeling negative**
   Result: agitated, irritable, stressed
3. **Low energy, feeling negative**
   Result: depressed, tired, lethargic
4. **Low energy, feeling positive**
   Result: calm, relaxed, peaceful.

You can work out your mood at this moment, just by assessing out how much energy you have and how positive or negative you feel, and mark this point on the map.

Concentration needs a specific mood, depending on the task. Generally people need sufficient energy to focus but not so much that they get distracted, and to feel relaxed enough but not lethargic. Mark your concentration point on your map,

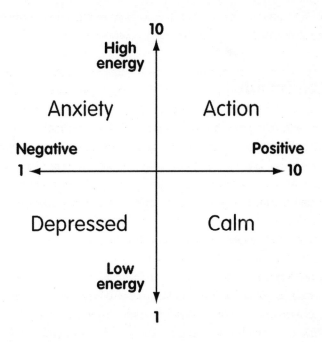

and aim to get your mood to that point whenever you want to concentrate. This may mean you have to sometimes think about your timing, your surroundings, your physical state and the sort of person you are when it comes to planning your approach to improving your personal art of concentration.

You may, for instance, feel quite low in energy, but positive, so this might be a good time to concentrate on something that isn't too demanding and wait until tomorrow morning, when a decent night's sleep could improve your energy, to go for a more demanding piece of work. Or you may be feeling rather negative, but high in energy, so your ability to concentrate might benefit from your taking twenty minutes' exercise, by walking briskly outside in the fresh air, to help stabilize your mood in preparation. Clarifying your mood can be very helpful in planning when to concentrate on particular tasks and when to take some time out to prepare for improved concentration.

And learning to manage your moods generally can, in the long term, improve your overall ability to concentrate.

Conclusion

○ **We may not be experts in concentration skills (yet), but the one thing we are all experts in is avoidance and procrastination,** particularly when we know we need to focus on something and give it our full attention. Learning to stop this bad habit is a good first step in learning how we can concentrate better on the task ahead.

○ **There are two types of distraction, internal and external, and neither of them is your friend when you want to concentrate better.** Internal distractions include the voice in your head (that constant, sniping, irritating, internal critic) or daydreaming, while external distractions include the telephone ringing, noises in the street and other people. The good news is that by learning the art of concentration, you can also learn to filter these distractions out.

○ **We learn to carry out lots of boring and routine tasks, such as washing the dishes or emptying the bins, on autopilot,** paying little attention to what we are doing and daydreaming of something more interesting. The trouble with autopilot is that it is counter-productive to learning and concentrating. You may get to the end of a chapter in your book and realize you haven't really retained any of the information you've just read. Learning how and when to use autopilot, and how to pay more attention to what you are doing right now will significantly help improve concentration skills.

○ **Negative thinking is another great distraction.** You're so busy telling yourself you cannot possibly do this job, finish reading that report or prepare a good presentation for your work colleagues that you use up all your energy convincing your-self that the task is a lost cause – even before you've started. The upshot? You've no energy left for concentrating on do-ing a good job. Identify your negative thoughts, see them for what they are, put them to one side and see how much better you are able to concentrate on what you need or want to accomplish.

○ **Try Mood Mapping** – it may help you identify what causes those moods that get in the way of concentration and, once you've identified them, help you see what steps you need to take to alleviate them.

CHAPTER FOUR
Your concentration profile

The brain is a wonderful organ. It starts working
the moment you get up in the morning and does
not stop until you get into the office.
Robert Frost

Are some people more naturally able to concentrate than others? Are some people just better at it – you may be one of them – and if so, why? You probably know people who are better at concentrating than others; they are less easily distracted, and more able to focus and absorb information. But is this because of how they are, or because they have learned better concentration skills? We all know 'butterfly brains' who simply flit from one thing to another, hardly able to retain a piece of information from one minute to the next, but is this how they were born or how they have become? Certainly, different personality types have different inclinations, or preferences, in how they approach life, and so when it comes to perfecting the art of concentration, it will be helpful to understand where you are starting from, what your natural inclination is and then, instead of fighting it, learn to work with your natural tendencies and aptitudes.

Gender differences

Research scientists, over recent years, have shown that there are gender differences, especially in early life, in the way we develop our ability to focus and concentrate. When it comes to extreme deficiencies in concentration skills, common in those with attention deficit disorders and autistic spectrum disorders, there is a marked gender predisposition, with a ratio of males to females diagnosed of around 4:1, although Dr Julia Rucklidge, from New Zealand's University of Canterbury's Department of Psychology, feels that there may also be cultural reasons for this. Her work suggests that there may be a referral bias when it comes to identifying ADHD in girls, and also that symptoms may not be as evident in girls because gender differences in brain development may make some, like inappropriate physical activity for example, less apparent.

Less well studied are those gender differences within the 'normal' range. In one of a very few studies based on the general population, carried out in 1993 and led by Jack Naglieri, professor and director of the Center for Cognitive Development at the George Mason University in Virginia, in the US, researchers assessed four different components of attention – planning, attention, simultaneous and successive (known as the PASS model of cognitive assessment). By and large, girls were better at attending and planning than boys, but not so good when it came to simultaneous and successive measures. What is interesting about this is that planning is one area that responds well to deliberate improvement, and can actually be learned, thus aiding concentration skills.

There is also a female advantage during early life when it comes to learning to read and write: girls demonstrated a greater aptitude for growth in vocabulary during the toddler years, and identifying words verbally is a necessary precursor to the development of literary skills. Researchers found that at two years old, girls' vocabulary exceeded boys' by 115 words, without there being a difference in the amount of time the toddlers were talked to by their mothers. So the female brain is activated earlier for language and literacy development which, given how early education is skewed with a bias towards literacy, will put girls at an automatic, early advantage when it comes to learning to concentrate in infant school. The danger is that the more action-focused male brain struggles in early education, and the die gets cast.

The most dramatic difference between girls' and boys' brains is not in its structure but in the sequence of development of the various brain regions. The world's largest study of brain development in children, published by the journal *Neuroimage* in 2007 (entitled 'Sexual Dimorphism of Brain Developmental Trajectories during Childhood and Adolescence') and carried out by the National Institute of Health in the US, has demonstrated dramatic differences in brain development in girls compared with boys. The different regions of the brain develop in a different sequence, and at a different rate. Girls' brains reach their inflection point (halfway point of development) at around the age of eleven, and boys at around the age of fifteen. This is one of the most significant new insights into brain development over the last few years.

'How long can you sit still, be quiet and pay attention?' asks Dr Leonard Sax, founder and executive director of the National Association for Single Sex Public Education in the US and author of *Why Gender Matters*.

If you compare 30-year-old men and 22-year-old women, you won't find dramatic differences in how long women and men can sit still, be quiet and pay attention. But ask the same question about 6-year-olds: how long can the

average 6-year-old boy sit still, be quiet and pay attention
– compared with the average 6-year-old girl? Most teachers
will tell you that the boy cannot sit still, be quiet and pay
attention nearly as long as the average 6-year-old girl. The
boy starts squirming, fidgeting, getting restless. He may
be diagnosed with attention deficit disorder; medication
may be prescribed. What those boys may really need is not
medication, but a better understanding that girls and boys
develop along different developmental trajectories. What
is developmentally appropriate for a 6-year-old girl may not
be developmentally appropriate for a 6-year-old boy.

There is a difference not only in the way that male and female
brains develop, but also in the way that male and female brains
are activated – sometimes for the same tasks. A study carried
out by researchers at Northwestern University in the US and the
University of Haifa in Israel in 2008 showed that boys and girls
activate different parts of the brain while performing the same
language tasks. Using functional MRI scanning, brain activity
was measured in both groups, in children aged between nine
and fifteen years old, while they carried out spelling and written language tasks. What the scientists discovered was that the
way the brain processed language was more abstract in girls,
and more sensory in boys. Even if the language task was auditory, rather than visual, the visual areas in the boys' brains lit
up, while this didn't occur among the girls. So the accuracy of
the boys depended on how hard the visual area of the brain was
working while doing the task.

While it's not yet clear why this gender difference occurs,
and scientists speculate it could date back to an evolutionary
advantage where survival required primitive man to recognize
dangerous sights and sounds very quickly, it does show that the
human brain can work in very different ways to achieve the
same task. This in part explains why different people, irrespective of their gender, have different learning styles. And different

VISUALIZATION EXERCISE

Start by looking at a familiar object. Look at its shape, its size, and the space around it and in relation to what is around it. This object could be a chair, or an apple. What it is doesn't much matter. You are not considering your relationship with it; you are just observing it and visualizing it. Don't get caught up in irrelevant thoughts about the object; just keep looking at it and really seeing it. Now think of six things you could say, or tell another person, about that object. The first time you try this you may hit six, but some people will struggle to reach four. Practise, and then move your target up to ten as you improve.

learning styles are worth knowing about because most of us have a natural preference for one or another, and this can make a difference to how we approach tasks, and how we can more successfully utilize concentration skills in a way that fits with our learning style.

Learning styles

Gender differences aside, when it comes to the ways in which we learn, we tend to vary between three distinct styles, and these become relevant to determining how we concentrate and the ways in which we find being able to concentrate either easy or more difficult. The theories behind this idea, put very simply, take into account the main ways in which we deal with information – the ways in which we perceive, process and organize it. And, when it comes to how we perceive information, the three different learning styles have been defined as visual, auditory and tactile (or kinaesthetic).

VISUAL LEARNERS

Visual learners tend towards seeing information in picture format and find it easiest to concentrate on information that is presented visually – diagrams, illustrated text books, overhead transparencies, videos, flipcharts and hand-outs. They tend to opt to sit at the front of the classroom, thus avoiding visual obstructions, such as other people's heads, and like to see the teacher's body language and facial expression to fully understand what they are being shown or taught. During lectures or discussions, visual learners often take detailed notes to help them concentrate on and absorb the information. They will often write a word out to remember how it is correctly spelled.

If you think you may be a visual learner, then the tips below may help you when it comes to concentrating:

○ Study in a quiet place, away from other visual disturbances.
○ Visualize any information as a picture.
○ Use visual media wherever possible.
○ Use pictures, charts and maps to help you focus.
○ Highlight texts and your own notes using colour.
○ Take notes, using headings and other 'signposts'.

AUDITORY LEARNERS

Auditory learners prefer to take in information through sound, rather than visual images. They tend to interpret the underlying 'meanings' of speech by listening to tone of voice, pitch, speed and other nuances, which means that for these types of learners written information may sometimes have little meaning until it is heard spoken out loud. Auditory learners often benefit from reading text aloud or using a tape recorder in order to help them concentrate on the information.

If you think you may be an auditory learner, then the tips below may help you when it comes to concentrating:

O Use a tape recorder if possible instead of (or as well as) making notes.
O Read text out loud.
O Record your ideas and listen to them played back.
O Create musical jingles and mnemonics to aid memory.
O Discuss your ideas verbally.
O Dictate to someone else while they write your ideas down.

TACTILE LEARNERS

Tactile learners learn best through a hands-on approach, actively exploring the physical world around them. They may find it hard to sit still and concentrate on information that is delivered in either an auditory or a visual form; they need to experience it to focus, and if they do have to sit for long periods they may become distracted by their need for activity and exploration. They need to move, touch and do things physically in order to focus and concentrate.

So if you think you may be a tactile learner, then the tips below may help you when it comes to concentrating:

O Take frequent breaks when working; concentrate in short bursts.
O Stand up to work.
O Move around while concentrating on new things. For example, read while using an exercise bike, or work out new concepts with models.
O Use bright colours to highlight reading material.
O Skim read before reading in detail.

When it comes to learning styles, while we may have a natural preference of one for another, that's not to say that we are stuck with it; and it may be that the challenge of trying one of the alternative approaches to learning will help when you are concentrating on developing a new skill. So if you find that

> ### ◎ MIND MAPS
>
> A mind map is a useful, graphic tool for thinking through, problem solving and planning your ideas. Visual learners will probably use mind maps already, but for auditory and tactile learners, this can be a good way of extending your learning style. Start with a single word, or phrase, in the middle of a blank page; then create the map from other associated ideas, concepts and thoughts, emphasizing different areas of importance. Then extrapolate from your mind map what you need to actively focus on for the task in hand.

concentrating is difficult when you use one learning style, then experiment with another. If you normally think of yourself as a visual learner, you will probably draw mind maps and use coloured highlighters to help you focus on, analyse or memorize information. But if you are getting stale, you may find it helpful to try a totally different approach, such as reading some text while you walk around the room, which is a tactile approach, or reading or singing it aloud, which is an auditory approach.

Personality types

It's obvious, just from looking around at the people we know, love or work with, that personalities differ. When it comes to definitions of personality types, there are numerous models. The first person to really think about this in the twentieth century was Carl Jung, who published his theories in 1921 in his book *Psychological Types*. However, his ideas were very psychoanalytical and abstract, and not terribly useful outside the consulting room and in everyday life. It took the mother-and-daughter team of Katherine Briggs and her daughter Isabel Myers, an American psychological theorist, to work through this and devise what became known as the Myers-Briggs Type Indicators (MBTI). This form of psychometric testing remains in use to this day, and is often used as the basis of decision making for job selection or careers advice; if you've had experience of these, then MBTI, or some variation of it, has probably been utilized.

Myers and Briggs were very clear that there was nothing right or wrong about an individual's psychological make-up, but what these personality indicators provided was an objective indication of preferences – the way of responding to something that an individual was most comfortable with, even if they could also manage or learn other ways of responding. It's important to remember that MBTI does not measure aptitude: it measures preferences. So it could be a useful way of looking at how you might prefer to apply your energies when needing to concentrate or focus.

Jung's original theory suggested that there were two main ways of thinking, rational or irrational, and these could be further broken down into 'judging' functions, thinking and feeling (rational), and 'perceiving' functions, sensing and intuition (irrational). In addition, these would be expressed differently, depending on whether the individual was an introvert or an extrovert.

This brings us to the four basic ways in which we prefer to approach things. Myers and Briggs took all this information and came up with the following model, and a group of eight descriptive terms, which were:

E	Extrovert	*or*	**I**	Introvert
S	Sensing	*or*	**N**	iNtuition
T	Thinking	*or*	**F**	Feeling
J	Judging	*or*	**P**	Perceiving

EXTROVERT OR INTROVERT?

Jung believed that, when it came to personality types, we tend towards being either extrovert or introvert. Those with an extrovert preference are energized by action and interaction, while introverts tend to be energized by internal thought. Extroverts tend to take action first and then reflect, while introverts tend towards reflecting first and then taking action.

SENSING OR INTUITING?

Sensing and intuiting are two ways in which information is gathered. Those whose preference is for sensing are more likely to trust information that is in the present, tangible and concrete – that is, information that can be understood by the five senses. They tend to distrust hunches that seem to come out of nowhere, preferring to look for details and facts. When it comes to those whose preference is for intuiting, they are more likely to trust information that is more abstract or theoretical, and they are more likely than those whose preference is for sensing to trust those flashes of insight that seem to come from nowhere.

THINKING OR FEELING?

Thinking and feeling are the decision-making preferences used about information gathered – whether by sensing or intuiting. Those who prefer thinking tend to decide things from a more detached standpoint, deciding on the basis of what seems reasonable, logical, causal and consistent. Those whose preference is for feeling tend to come to decisions by looking at the situation with more empathy, and weighing it up to achieve the most harmony and consensus for all concerned.

JUDGING OR PERCEIVING?

These two categories refer to our preferences for the way in which we choose to live and so, therefore, influence our lifestyle choices. Those whose preference is for judging tend towards an organized, planned way of life, while those for whom a perceiving preference is more comfortable tend towards a more spontaneous, flexible way of going about life.

Personality-type combinations

The possible combinations of four of these four variants from each of the main groups create sixteen basic personality-type combinations: ISTJ; ISFJ; INFJ; INTJ; ISTP; ISFP; INFP; INTP; ESTP; ESFP; ENFP; ENTP; ESTJ; ESFJ; ENFJ; ENTJ.

In the abstract, this is just a string of letters representing the either/or preferences in the four groups, and won't initially mean much, but looking more closely makes the information more relevant. Remember that the demarcation of personality types is just an indication of preferences, and these are not set in stone. What may be helpful, though, is the identification of new ways of trying to focus and concentrate that could be more in tune with your preferences.

ISTJ Introvert; Sensing; Thinking; Judging
ISTJ-type personalities value thoroughness, and like detailed, objective information on which they can concentrate. They dislike distractions and are comfortable working alone, with a tendency to prefer machines, facts and numbers to people. They can sometimes be over-concerned with detail, but tend to be well-motivated, hard workers.

ISFJ Introvert; Sensing; Feeling; Judging
ISFJs are comfortable with sequential procedures and like to work towards tangible results, preferring to take their time to do everything to perfection. They prefer minimal interruptions and need little supervision, being highly self-determined, and like to focus on one thing at a time.

INFJ Introvert; iNtuiting; Feeling; Judging
INFJ types are often very single minded, but highly creative, thinking things through carefully and with good concentration, disliking distractions. Because of an active inner life, they have a preference for working in well-organized settings that support their concentration, but want to organize their own time.

INTJ Introvert; iNtuiting; Thinking; Judging

INTJs prefer to have a very clear idea in their own minds about their goals, and tend towards working in very logical and orderly ways. Because they like to visualize how things may work out, they can be very strategic and good at devising theoretical models for what they want to achieve.

ISTP Introvert; Sensing; Thinking; Perceiving

ISTP types tend to be great observers, but can get restless if not challenged. They are very curious, but dislike ambiguity and unnecessary details, and tend towards problem solving in a very systematic way, while retaining facts and details very easily (as long as they are of interest to them).

ISFP Introvert; Sensing; Feeling; Perceiving

ISFPs often come across as very likeable, quiet and modest types, idealists who prefer to work behind the scenes. They can be highly motivated when focusing on something they care about, but can sometimes become overwhelmed by indecision, which can make organization a problem.

INFP Introvert; iNtuiting; Feeling; Perceiving

INFPs tend to dislike schedules and deadlines, preferring to do things their own way, and can have trouble working in competitive environments. They tend to go about complex tasks in a quiet, inauspicious way, and prefer not to reveal too much about their inner life to others.

INTP Introvert; iNtuiting; Thinking; Perceiving

INTPs have a preference towards working independently and setting their own goals in a flexible environment; and while they enjoy developing concepts and complex models and systems, they prefer to hand over the implementation of these to others. Good on detail, they are not so good at articulating their ideas in a way that others can understand.

ESTP Extrovert; Sensing; Thinking; Perceiving

ESTPs tend towards being very logical and results-oriented, but also thrive on tight deadlines and chaos. They enjoy having a lot of projects on the go at once, have a lot of energy and can sometimes be rather blunt, but they are always good in a crisis.

ESFP Extrovert; Sensing; Feeling; Perceiving

ESFPs can be very spontaneous, and often leave things to the last minute, preferring variety and lots of different projects to juggle, which can sometimes impede their follow-through. As they prefer to be action-oriented, sitting still and concentrating can sometimes take discipline.

ENFP Extrovert; iNtuiting; Feeling; Perceiving

ENFPs prefer lots of variety, and are good at starting things but less good at finishing them. They enjoy working collaboratively, and thinking on their feet. Good at creative solutions to problems, they are less good at the detail, and lack of concentration in that area can cause difficulties.

ENTP Extrovert; iNtuiting; Thinking; Perceiving

ENTP types can have difficulty focusing, because so many things are interesting to them. They thrive on imaginative ideas, and are very good at the initiation of projects but less good at the follow-through; they use ingenuity to solve problems, and enjoy juggling numerous ideas at the same time.

ESTJ Extrovert; Sensing; Thinking; Judging

ESTJs tend to prefer being in charge, finding it easier to concentrate when they are problem solving and taking calculated risks, and then moving on. They are excellent organizers – people, places, things – and they use time well to try to achieve tangible results. Can get a bit impatient with others when things are slow or sloppy.

ESFJ Extrovert; Sensing; Feeling; Judging

ESFJs like schedules and routines, and dislike dealing with things that are too abstract. They thrive on contact with others, are good team players and tend towards being conscientious and diligent. Can be very social, caring a great deal about how others see them – but their parties are always well planned.

ENFJ Extrovert; iNtuiting; Feeling; Judging

ENFJs tend towards being decisive, well organized and goal-oriented, but can get frustrated by slow progress. They prefer having control, and running their own projects, and can accept setbacks as challenges. Good at motivating others, they are natural leaders and good communicators.

ENTJ Extrovert; iNtuiting; Thinking; Judging

ENTJ types are very energetic and competent. They tend to see obstacles as challenges and like to be ahead of schedule when it comes to getting things done. They prefer to be well organized and are results-driven, tending towards goal setting and strategic ways of working.

Although this is a very brief introduction to a very complex way of analysing personality types – and if you are interested, you can find out more and have your Myers-Briggs Type Indicator professionally assessed – you can see that different personality types will have very different approaches when it comes to concentrating on something. This is why it's worth getting a handle on how you operate, which you can then use to your advantage, rather than constantly battling against it. You may have read, for example, that listening to loud music will help you concentrate. Well, it might, if you are working with your natural predisposition, but if not – well, you're likely to find it very distracting and it will prevent you from concentrating well.

Convergent/divergent thinkers

Convergent or divergent thinking styles were identified by American cognitive psychologist J.P. Guilford, best remembered for his psychometric study of human intelligence, and were part of his model for the structure of the intellect. He made a distinction between two very different ways of problem solving, and from his research suggested that we tend to be one or the other when it comes to the way in which we think in order to solve problems.

Convergent thinking is a way of finding the one single, best answer to a problem. Divergent thinking is the creative production of multiple answers to a problem. Both styles of thinking have their place, and can work well together, but as Guilford found, individuals will display a strong preference towards one type of thinking over the other. Generally speaking, scientists and engineer types tend towards convergent thinking, and artists and performers tend towards divergent thinking. When it comes to identifying the sum of the internal angles of a triangle, for example, where there is only one possible answer, then convergent thinking works best. But if you want to find ten possible uses for a piece of string, then divergent thinking works better.

This becomes particularly relevant to concentration when there is a clash in your preferred way of thinking and the task in hand. If you are, by nature, a divergent thinker, then concentrating on single-answer tasks can quickly become boring and it would be easy to become distracted. In the same way, trying to concentrate on a task that requires a degree of creative thinking won't come so easily to a convergent thinker. Bearing this in mind, if your way of thinking is at odds with the task on which you want to concentrate, it may be useful to consider ways to make the task more easily achievable.

⊕ HOW DO YOU CONCENTRATE BEST?

1. **When you have a piece of work to do, do you**
   a) Prepare well in advance, and complete before
      your deadline *(1 point)*
   b) Make a lot of notes from which you can work *(3)*
   c) Think and talk about it to others before you start work *(4)*
   d) Leave it to the last minute *(2)*

2. **Is your workspace**
   a) Uncluttered and without unnecessary objects *(4)*
   b) Clear, apart from what you need for the job *(2)*
   c) A small space cleared in the middle of a lot of clutter *(3)*
   d) You don't have a workspace *(1)*

3. **When you are working, do you prefer**
   a) Total silence *(3)*
   b) Some background noise *(2)*
   c) Music *(4)*
   d) Any of these – you're indifferent to noise *(1)*

4. **When you are using the phone**
   a) Do you usually use your right ear *(4)*
   b) Do you usually use your left ear *(3)*
   c) Do you use alternate ears *(1)*
   d) Do you prefer to use a hands-free set and move around *(2)*

5. **Do you use the phone mainly**
   a) To gossip *(4)*
   b) For work calls *(1)*
   c) To exchange the bare minimum of information *(3)*
   d) As little as possible *(2)*

▶

6. How often do you turn off your mobile phone

a) Never *(4 points)*

b) When I am not at work, so in the evenings
and weekends *(2)*

c) When I go to bed *(3)*

d) I don't have a mobile phone *(1)*

7. When you read, do you

a) Consciously read every word as if you can
hear it in your head *(3)*

b) Mouth the words as you read *(4)*

c) Make notes as you read *(2)*

d) Skim read *(1)*

8. In order not to forget something, do you

a) Write yourself a note *(3)*

b) Repeat it over and over again to remind yourself *(4)*

c) Put an object somewhere strange to remind you *(2)*

d) None of these – you never forget *(1)*

9. In order to find a solution to a problem, do you

a) Think of lots of different ways around it *(4)*

b) Immediately see one way and find out how to do it *(3)*

c) Panic *(1)*

d) Ask someone for help *(2)*

10. When working on a project, do you prefer

a) To work alone *(3)*

b) To work with one or two people *(1)*

c) To lead a team *(4)*

d) To provide your expertise as back-up to a team *(2)*

▶

SCORES

10–15 points: You're pretty easy going and don't have much of a preference for how you approach things, but you may find that some things are easier to concentrate on than others. Thinking about what comes more naturally to you, and identifying it, may help you find new and different ways to approach old problems if you feel you have got rather stuck in your ways.

15–25 points: You have a tendency towards being a hands-on sort of person. You find it easier to concentrate if something makes physical sense to you, so you like to work things out by moving around, looking at things from different angles and being able to touch things. You probably have good spatial abilities and approach things from different angles, with a preference towards divergent thinking. You enjoy being good at what you do and are happy to add your expertise to a team or work alone.

25–35 points: Your preference is towards a visual approach to learning. You probably doodle when you're on the phone, and like to work things out by drawing diagrams or flow charts and making lists. You can strengthen your listening skills to balance this, but you tend to remember things by picturing them, and can be a very good speller because you can 'see' the words in your head.

35–40 points: Your preference is what you hear, and you are probably good at concentrating on what you hear. You may also be a good linguist, mimic or musician. However, you can balance this by drawing on additional ways to help you concentrate: don't rely just on what you've heard when you're trying to improve your concentration, but make a note as well.

Conclusion

O **Why are some people butterfly brained? And why can others stay focused and concentrate while the house falls down around their ears?** Are we all just born differently or does personality have an impact on your ability to concentrate? The answer is yes and no, because while some people have more of a natural aptitude for concentrating, everyone can learn to improve their concentration skills. But before you start, work out what personality type you are so that you work with your natural inclinations, not against them.

O **As well as personality types, people have different learning styles.** Again, it's worth working out which one you favour so that you can harness this aptitude as a strength to help you improve your ability to concentrate. The three different types of learning are visual, auditory and tactile (or kinaesthetic). Work out which way you learn and you will know what props you need to boost your powers of concentration.

O **Take the quiz on page 97 and work out your concentration profile right now.** Do you need to find new and different ways to approach old problems and improve your ability to concentrate until you've found a solution? Are you the hands-on type who needs to feel and touch something to really understand it, or are you a more visual person who needs to develop their listening skills to enable you to concentrate better on what others are saying? The quiz will help you decide what works best for you and which areas you need to work on to become better at concentrating.

CHAPTER FIVE

What do you need to help you concentrate?

I believe attention is the most powerful tool of the human spirit. We can enhance or augment our attention with practices like meditation and exercise, diffuse it with technologies like email and BlackBerries, or alter it with pharmaceuticals. In the end, though, we are fully responsible for how we choose to use this extraordinary tool.

Linda Stone

Marie Curie, the Polish scientist born in 1867 who won two Nobel prizes, for physics in 1903 and for chemistry in 1911, was the youngest of five children. There is an apocryphal story about her as a child, being so engrossed in reading a book that she didn't notice her siblings mischievously stacking a canopy of dining-room chairs over her head until she finished the book, stood up and brought the chairs cascading down. Her ability to concentrate was either part of her personality or well developed and enhanced by her passion for science. Either way, it stood her in good stead for a life of scientific exploration and discovery.

We don't know whether she was born able to concentrate, but we do know that because of her interest in science, she was happily inclined towards spending time immersing herself in the subject. And that's one of the keys to concentration: having a genuine interest in a subject and, if it's not intrinsically interesting, finding a way to make it interesting enough to enable us to continue concentrating. Some of us will find this harder than others.

Familiarity v. novelty

It's a subtle balance between something that is not so familiar as to be boring, and something that is not so new that there is no point of reference, in order to hold our concentration. Consider how a young child's concentration can be held by something that is familiar but does something novel: an adult he knows pulling a funny face will make him laugh. But also consider how the amusement will pall after a period of time or, if someone unknown pulls a funny face, then this might alarm him or make him cry. In adult life, we like our challenges to be manageable, but once they become too manageable, they are no longer challenges. So the trick is to choose tasks or activities that are at the edge of our competence, and which force us to concentrate. If a task is too easy we lose focus and become bored, and if it's too hard we feel overwhelmed and unable to concentrate.

Commitment

What does this mean, and how can it help you to concentrate? Making a firm commitment to what you want to do can make concentration easier, because you are then investing a process with some value that is beneficial to you. Evaluating your personal commitment to a task will also be helped by looking at the beneficial outcome, or reward for what you do – and this, in turn, will help motivate commitment. Without this kind of commitment, a task can seem laborious and unfulfilling, which makes concentration more difficult. But if you are convinced of a positive outcome that will be rewarding or fun, then it becomes less difficult to concentrate. For example, if you need to concentrate on learning the Highway Code, because you want to take your driving test, pass and be able to drive, then the long-term beneficial outcome of being able to drive for the rest of your life is obvious, weighed against the short-term investment of concentrating on learning the rules and the necessity of knowing them in order to be able to drive safely.

Commitment is less straightforward if the benefits of concentration are cumulative, or not immediately evident. The concentration necessary to get homework done, when the benefits aren't immediately obvious, can make concentration – on Latin declension endings, for example – difficult, to say the least. This is when it becomes useful to consider some short-term goals, smaller steps on which you can build. If you can find some way of enjoying the process too, then the commitment to the short-term goal, and its possible long-term outcome, becomes easier.

Without concentration, a restless mind dissipates a lot of energy. We know that without concentration, something that need take you only an hour takes you two (or more!); worse than that, you feel fatigued and irritated by the process of doing it. You have wasted energy frittering away time – time that you could have used to better advantage. A restless mind can also wander off into negative thought patterns, and if you need just one reason to convince you it is worthwhile taking steps to improve your concentration skills, this is it.

Enthusiasm

We all know how easy it is to concentrate on something we're interested in and have an enthusiasm or passion for. Time flies when you're having fun, as the saying goes, but the same time really drags if you are trying to concentrate on something you find boring. And enthusiasm is important, because it enhances motivation – another key factor in helping make concentration easier. So how can you muster more enthusiasm? Take a look at something you enjoy, and have enthusiasm for, and work out why. Is it because you know a lot about it, and are interested in knowing more? Is it because doing it makes you feel better about yourself in some way, or it gives you a sense of ownership or pride? If you can identify what you do in order to become enthusiastic about something, apply it elsewhere.

For anyone new to the plays of Shakespeare, for example, the old-fashioned use of language and the long-winded way of telling a story doesn't make his writing immediately accessible – hence you will hear many people professing that they don't like Shakespeare, and often they will say they don't like it because it's boring. Without a context or an understanding of what he was trying to achieve, Shakespeare's plays and sonnets can seem like a load of gobbledegook at first – especially in contrast to how most of us experience dramatic storytelling today, with fast-action plots and computer-generated special effects. In comparison, there seems little to hold the attention. However, take a play like *Romeo and Juliet*, with its timeless theme of girl meets boy, and then look at a popular TV soap like *EastEnders*, *Neighbours*, *Friends* or *The Simpsons*, and you can see what similarities in themes or points of reference there are – boy meets girl is one of the commonest. Whatever the drama, it addresses human themes. But watching a one-off episode of a TV soap isn't in itself very interesting in the first five minutes: you don't know who the characters are, what their role is or what the backstory is. Stay with it, however, and you get a context and a scenario which you can engage with, form opinions on, react to – by which stage, you have an interest in what's happening. It's the same with one of Shakespeare's plays. Just by giving it a little time, you will have gained enough information to connect to it. And that's when it starts to get interesting. You might then find you have enough enthusiasm to stay with it for long enough to really concentrate on it. Finally, you are concentrating enough to get something out of it, which then makes further concentration easier; and so it continues.

It doesn't matter what the subject is – football, world economics, history homework or your tax return: nothing is inherently interesting until you gain some information which you can engage with, focus on, concentrate on and even enjoy. Otherwise it really is just boring. This is a process that can be brought to bear on anything on which you want to concentrate better. Once you have made a start, stay with it, and something positive will begin to emerge which makes it easier to stay focused for longer periods. Build on this process, and eventually you will find something to be enthusiastic about because you have made the effort to invest it with some meaning for yourself, and thus made it more relevant and more interesting to you. Given how often we have to do things that are mundane, repetitive and tedious, then knowing that we can find ways to make them meaningful to us means we will start to find them easier to concentrate on and accomplish.

Whether Marie Curie was born with an inherent interest in science or not, something or someone sparked her interest, and she was able to nurture it even if there were times when she too had to push through barriers of boredom or frustration. She would have been able to do this, and keep going, because by this time, she had enough enthusiasm for the topic to help her concentrate on the difficult parts until the next interesting bit.

I once coached a student who had to read Charles Dickens' *Great Expectations* – a book he had zero interest in but that was important for his GCSE coursework. He never read for pleasure, couldn't see the point of books and looked with horror at the sheer thickness of this classic, unable to begin to work out how he was going to plough his way through it. It seemed a shame to me that he should have to read this book without getting any sense of enjoyment out of it, so between us we worked out a strategy as to how he might accomplish his task and ac-

FIVE MORE RULE

Sam Horn, communications and creativity consultant, and author of *ConZentrate: Get Focused and Pay Attention*, recommends the 'Five More Rule'. She says:

There are two kinds of people. Those who have learned how to work through frustration, and those who wish they had. From now on, if you're in the middle of a task and tempted to give up – just do five more. **Read *five more* pages. Finish *five more* maths problems. Work *five more* minutes.**

Just as athletes build physical stamina by pushing past the point of exhaustion, you can build mental stamina by pushing past the point of frustration. And just as runners get their second wind by not giving up when their body initially protests, you can get your 'second mind' by not giving up when your willpower initially protests. Continuing to concentrate when your brain is tired is the key to stretching your attention span and building mental endurance.

tually get something worthwhile from the experience, which might even make him want to read more.

First, I asked him for his suggestions, and he said he would read one chapter a day during his half-term break from school. Seven days and seven chapters, out of a total of fifty-nine – the book has very short chapters – were not going to get him very far. In addition, a chapter a day wasn't going to be enough for him to get into the story, engage with it and start to have an interest in it. How about reading for just half an hour a day, I suggested – could he manage that? This was our agreement and his goal, and I hoped it would help him get into the book enough to enjoy it. When we next met, I asked him how he'd got on and was delighted to discover that he had read the whole book over the half-term break. He had found that reading for long enough meant that he got into the book, engaged with the plot and characters, and wanted to find out more. His enthusiasm for the story motivated him to keep reading. And not only was he pleased with himself for doing so, but he realized that he liked reading after all – not all the time, of course, but it no longer felt like a boring thing that he had to do just to get his schoolwork done.

Slow down

One of the by-products of our overactive, multitasking lifestyles is that we often attempt to get everything done as fast as possible, because we have so much to do and because of the pressure of work. Modern technology has created a do-it-now mentality to which we can become almost addicted because the release of those stress hormones that create a speedy, heightened sense of awareness becomes the 'norm'. We begin to think this is how we should feel, and subconsciously we seek to generate this state of being because we have come to associate this feeling with achievement. But when we do things fast, we tend not to concentrate as well, and mistakes can be made. Whether this means sending an email and forgetting the attachment, oversalting a recipe, minor car accidents, leaving the house without your keys or forgetting a meeting with a friend, the undisputable fact is that when we are distracted by this self-imposed busy-ness, we make errors of judgement and forget things. Slowing down not only allows time for concentration, but also makes concentration more possible, and helps you get into the habit of concentrating on one thing at a time.

This is not about reducing the rate at which you work to that of a tortoise rather than a hare – for many people that would be counter-intuitive and counterproductive. It's more about noticing how you rush things to get them done, and how you could take a little more time without losing out and, in reality, even find you are achieving more. We often get into habits that, on examination, don't do us any favours. Sometimes we are so fixed on the achievement, the outcome of what we are doing, that we forget about the process of doing it and the importance of doing it well and with enjoyment. Slowing down isn't just about avoiding mistakes, but about being in the moment and allowing ourselves to feel the pleasure of that. The more we do this, the less likely we are to evoke the sort of stress that has become commonplace in today's society, with its emphasis on all that high-speed, multitasking activity.

Slowing down, momentarily, between tasks can also help enhance concentration skills. Taking a moment to mentally 'sign off' from one thing before moving on to another, and deliberately paying attention to what you've just been doing, allows the brain to focus and complete the process. This also has the advantage of committing to memory what you have just concluded, making it easier to remember where you were with it – for example, where you put something when you went to answer the phone – and will then save you time when you return later to the task.

Hearing and listening

We hear with our ears, but we listen with our brains. Hearing is passive, while listening is an active process. How many times have you been 'listening' to what someone was saying to you, but you've hardly heard a word because your mind was elsewhere? You were distracted. You were not really concentrating. Active listening helps concentration. Active listening also encourages the person who is speaking, so can be a useful skill for other reasons.

Another contributory factor to listening is which ear is dominant. We tend to favour the use of one ear over another, and you may notice that you always use one ear rather than

⦿ KEY POINTERS FOR ACTIVE LISTENING

- Focus with your eyes on the person speaking.
- Think about what they are saying.
- If your attention wanders, bring it back to what is being spoken about.
- Make mental notes of key points as you listen.
- Make written notes of key points, but don't attempt to write everything down.
- You should be able to repeat back, in your own words, the gist of what is being said.
- Make affirmative but silent movements, to acknowledge to the speaker that you are listening.

the other when you answer the phone. There may be a number of reasons for this, which may include habit, better hearing in one ear or the ease with which you can raise your arm. But it may be because you are right-ear or left-ear dominant. Whatever the case, there is an argument that says you should use your right ear if you are wanting to concentrate – or talk into someone else's right ear if you want them to concentrate on what you are saying – because this exploits something that is known as right-ear advantage, which was first identified in the 1960s by Doreen Kimura, an expert in the neurobiology of cognition and visiting professor at the Simon Fraser University in Canada.

The thinking behind right-ear advantage is that because the right ear is directly connected to the left brain, the side of the brain that processes language, there is a direct, fast connection. If you listen with your left ear, the sounds first go to the right brain, and because this has to be rerouted to the left side of the brain via the *corpus callosum* the information has to follow a longer pathway and is delayed. Of course this delay is in nanoseconds but the right-ear advantage may have some bearing on how well we concentrate on what we hear. And it appears that right-ear dominant people tended to find learning easier.

The benefits of boredom

Being bored can, surprisingly, be a motivating factor, if it spurs you on to find out things for yourself, and gain enough information to make something more interesting. This is why it's crucial for children to experience boredom, so that they can then find within themselves the self-motivation to create interest. Parents often seem to fear their child's boredom, perhaps because they see it as a waste of time, or because they worry that their offspring may waste that time even further, possibly by getting into mischief. Children's lives today are constantly being filled up with activity, which is often more meaningful to the adult than to the child who has to participate in it.

The downside of all this activity is that it's difficult to learn how to manage feelings of boredom comfortably, and work through them, rather than distract ourselves from them. The habit of constantly seeking distraction from boredom can be counterproductive to learning how to concentrate. Without the experience of being bored, we are unlikely to actively seek ways to make something less boring. The child who finds reading boring and automatically seeks something of immediate interest and gratification, rather than continuing to read for long enough to engage with the story and get to the point where it does become interesting to them, can be a casualty of this 'must fill every minute with activity' mindset. Learning that boredom is a precursor to finding something on which to concentrate, or focus attention, is an important stage of intellectual development, the development of curiosity that will make an interest in just about anything possible, and concentration an inevitable consequence.

You can witness this at work in young babies: they are curious about everything, and as they explore something, their attention is held and their concentration is obvious. Constant distraction from this process makes boredom obsolete, but also has the unwanted side effect of diminishing the capacity for curiosity. Constant distraction can also become habit-forming, and in itself hamper concentration. Boredom can therefore sometimes be a powerful and underestimated tool.

Giving something meaning makes it easier to concentrate

It is also much easier to focus and concentrate on something that has meaning for us. For example, remembering a random series of letters can be tricky. Try it:

H D S O A W H D H A G F A T K H A A T K M C P H T A

However hard you concentrate, there seems to be no rhyme or reason to the sequence of letters to make it stick in your mind. But once you know that the letters stand for the words of a well-known children's nursery rhyme, it becomes easier: 'Humpty Dumpty sat on a wall;/Humpty Dumpty had a great fall./All the King's horses and all the King's men,/Couldn't put Humpty together again.'

When it comes to concentrating on something, it's much easier if the task has meaning for you and is something you can engage with. Often, concentration becomes easier once you have been concentrating for a while, because what it is you are concentrating on starts to have greater meaning for you, the longer you concentrate on it. Even watching a movie requires you to watch it for long enough to engage with its content. Reading a book is the same. It's unusual to engage fully with the first few pages – people talk about 'getting into a book' or a book being 'difficult to get into' – but, as we have seen, if you continue reading long enough, the brain engages with the content and concentration becomes easier. So if concentration is elusive, continuing with a task until some meaning has been created with which you can engage will definitely help. For some, this simple lesson is so easily learned that it appears to come naturally; for others, it takes time and practice to learn how effective it can be.

This process works because by giving information meaning you recruit an additional part of your brain, the left inferior prefrontal cortex. Short-term memory, which we use for immediate repetition, lasts for only about fifteen seconds and can really manage only around seven bits of information at one time (which hardly encourages concentration). Continuing long enough with a task until it becomes meaningful will significantly help concentration. What's more, the task will be automatically stored in our mind and be remembered for much longer – which explains why concentrating long enough to make information meaningful can be so beneficial to everyday life, whatever we do.

Skill level v. task demands

Have you ever tried to do something and discovered you didn't know what you were doing? Or started a task without fully understanding what you needed to do? Or agreed to do something while knowing that you were not fully equipped to do so? Driving a car without knowing exactly where you are going, for instance, or trying to assemble a piece of flat-pack furniture before having read through all the instructions. It's difficult to concentrate on what you are trying to do – drive the car safely or match the right screw to the right hole – if there are gaps in your information. Not having the right skills for the task can also give rise to anxiety or frustration, which can also impair concentration. This is when you are taken beyond your level of competence and the task becomes overwhelming. You can't concentrate. At this point, you need to take a step back, ask for help, get some more information or try in a different way.

It becomes counterproductive to push on without gathering the wherewithal to do so.

Equally, if a task is below your competence, then you will find it difficult to engage too. It will bore you and you are likely to switch off. The ideal is for a task to be at the very edge of your competence and ability, so that there is also a level of challenge. Utilizing the skills you have but raising the bar on your capability will create a challenge. So, if you have to do something you have done before, time and time again, and feel insufficiently challenged, then do it differently. Find a way to extend your skills, or make it just difficult enough to force you to focus. Build on that. This will help you concentrate better.

Emotional, physical and psychological state

The image of the starving, love-struck poet in the freezing garret, turning out exquisite verse, is a highly romanticized view of what it is possible to achieve in adverse conditions. In reality, concentration comes more easily if you are in a good physical and psychological state, where your emotions are even and you are feeling upbeat and positive. Very few people have their concentration levels enhanced by adversity (unless you are concentrating on escaping that sabre-toothed tiger), when other processes, triggered by the 'fight or flight' hormones, come into play. However, when you are feeling happy and at peace, and not preoccupied with the trials and tribulations of the world, concentration comes more easily.

According to Mihaly Csikszentmihalyi, professor of psychology and education at the Claremont Graduate University in the US:

Negative emotions like sadness, fear, anxiety or boredom can produce 'psychic entropy' in the mind. That is a state in which we cannot use attention effectively to deal with external tasks because we need to restore an inner subjective order. Positive emotions like happiness, strength, or alertness are states of 'psychic negentropy' because we don't need attention to ruminate and feel sorry for ourselves, and psychic energy can flow freely into whatever thought or task we choose to invest it in.

Of course it's completely unrealistic to expect life to be harmonious 100 per cent of the time; it's just not like that. Inevitably we have days when we feel down or mess up. However, it is possible to exacerbate how we feel with bad habits that come from constantly overworking, not eating properly, not sleeping enough or allowing other things or people constantly to distract us. Perpetuating this state of affairs will inevitably diminish your ability to concentrate, and maybe also lead to long-term problems with anxiety and depression. If you think that your impaired concentration is part of a bigger problem that can't be completely alleviated through self-management (improved diet, exercise, better sleep), then seek help. Whether you need some short-term medication, cognitive behavioural therapy or therapeutic assistance, it is worth asking for help if you recognize that the very quality of your life is becoming impaired.

Environment

When it comes to the environment in which you are trying to concentrate, it's important to bear in mind how far your surroundings can intrude on your capacity for concentration. Being too hot or too cold will immediately have an impact if you are uncomfortably one or the other. If there is a lot of noise, or too much visual stimulus, this may also distract you. Some people (like Marie Curie, it would seem) can block everything out so successfully that their concentration is unimpaired by the activity around them. The rest of us find that more difficult. While it is possible to adapt to a certain amount of distraction, and learn how to filter it out and prevent it from encroaching on our concentration, for most of us this is a tricky balance. When something is innately interesting, we aren't tired or hungry and there is a calm external environment, then concentration is easier.

For one person, complete quiet is an aid to concentration; for others, background music can help. While the Google workplace, which has won awards for being such a fun and friendly place to work in, may suit those who are by nature creative and gregarious, it might not suit others who like a little more peace and quiet. While some surgeons will perform intricate brain surgery to the thumping background strains of Guns 'n' Roses, others might prefer soothing Mozart – or absolute quiet. How far we are able to concentrate in particular environments is partly to do with what personality type we are, but also determined by a variety of other external factors. However, when practising the art of concentration, you might as well give yourself all the help you can get initially by opting for calm, comfortable surroundings that are free from distractions, before challenging yourself in different environments.

When it comes to your workplace environment, there are various basic considerations that can negatively impact on your productivity and health and, by extension, your concentration. If you can't concentrate on what you are trying to do, then it will take longer and you are also likely to be less accurate and, ultimately, less productive. If your environment somehow impinges on your health, or if it is too noisy and stressful to allow you to concentrate, these factors will also have a direct effect on productivity. So it makes sense to look at how your environment is affecting your concentration, and address it.

Ideally, any place where you want to spend some time concentrating should be clean and uncluttered. Even those who say that an untidy environment, particularly at work, is not a distraction to them will find – to a greater or lesser degree – that a tidy, organized environment is more conducive to tidy, organized and more effective concentration. Yes, great creative brains may still manage to spark off among last night's old apple cores and dirty coffee cups, but the rest of us usually need to focus on getting something done efficiently and accurately, and endless paraphernalia that takes up space can be impede this, so keep things simple.

Good lighting aids concentration, and full-spectrum lighting has been shown to be particularly helpful because it provides light that is the equivalent to natural daylight, which helps inhibit the secretion of melatonin from the pineal gland in the brain. Melatonin is the brain chemical that makes us sleepy, and in dull or inadequate light enough can be secreted, even during the day, to make you feel too drowsy to concentrate well. In addition, full-spectrum lighting doesn't flicker. Research has shown pretty conclusive evidence that full-spectrum lighting gives a benefit to those who suffer from seasonal affective disorder or SAD; and one study of adults with ADHD, carried out at the University of Toronto between November 2003 and February 2004, showed a significant decrease in both subjective and objective measures of core ADHD pathology and improved mood symptoms. Fluorescent lighting is very tiring on the eyes because it flickers constantly, albeit imperceptibly, which can make concentration difficult. So even if you only change the lighting in your work environment, this could make a huge difference to your ability to concentrate well.

Conclusion

O **Choosing activities or tasks that take you to the edge of your existing comfort level will really help your powers of concentration.** Something that is too familiar will quickly become boring, and you will stop concentrating on it. Something that is too big a challenge may deter you from having a go at all, so your concentration levels will stay stuck where they are. Take baby steps to push your powers of concentration that little bit further.

○ **It may sound contrary, but one of the best ways you can start to improve your ability to concentrate is not to crank up and do more but to slow down.** You cannot concentrate fully when you are rushing through a task. You're more likely to make mistakes and when the job is done you'll know you could have done it better, if only you had taken more time. Slowing down will also help you to learn to concentrate on one thing at a time and do it well, instead of doing half a dozen things badly.

○ **Giving something meaning will make it easier to concentrate on and, eventually, store it in your long-term memory for retrieval at a later date.** If you've heard people talk about it taking time to get into a book, what they mean is you have to invest time and effort and concentrate on the story and the characters to really engage in the book, by which time the tale will have meaning for you and you'll be able to concentrate on it.

CHAPTER SIX
Learning to concentrate

You need to let little things that would ordinarily
bore you suddenly thrill you.
Andy Warhol

True life is lived when tiny changes occur.
Leo Tolstoy

L ike any activity in which you want to make an improvement,
you need to take a structured approach and also discipline
yourself to be consistent in your efforts to improve your
concentration. There is absolutely no doubt at all that anyone
can improve their concentration, should they so choose. Making
that choice is the first step, and knowing how to take the subse-
quent steps will help you maintain the initial discipline and reap
the rewards that will encourage you to continue.

Timing
When trying to improve concentration skills, or to do exercises
or activities that will help improve them, it's worth thinking

about when you do so, because the timing can affect your application and also the effectiveness of your efforts. This is important, because if you don't manage to make a difference when you try, you will lose motivation. With any new activity, you need to make time initially to explore and extend your ability. Do not expect success if you attempt an improvement when you are overtired or feeling unwell, hungry or uncomfortable in some way. All these things will serve to distract you, so to start off with choose a time when you feel well rested, relaxed and comfortable and allocate a period of time without interruptions. Turn off the phone or switch the answer machine on. If you are at work, make sure your colleagues know that you are not to be interrupted for a while; if at home, ask your family not to disturb you for an hour. Also, choose a time that fits in with your own biological clock.

Circadian rhythms

We all have circadian rhythms that we can use to work to our advantage. Sometimes known as our 'biological clock', these are influenced by the light/dark cycle of the normal day, and regulated by the secretion of the hormone melatonin from the pineal gland, in response to light received via the eye. They also affect physiological aspects of our function such as core body temperature and blood pressure. For example, the sharpest rise in blood pressure is in the morning as we wake, testosterone secretion peaks in the morning and high alertness occurs at around 10.00, with best coordination at around 14.00 and fastest reaction times around an hour after that. Greatest cardiovascular and muscle strength occurs at around 17.00, and melatonin secretion begins at around 21.00, in response to dimming light. Deepest sleep occurs at around 02.00, and lowest body temperature occurs during sleep at around 04.00. This changing physiological cycle also affects other bodily functions. Bowel movements, for example, are suppressed at night and reactivated in the morning. Circadian rhythms aren't influenced so much by the 'cues' of daily life – mealtimes, patterns of wakefulness or sleeping, intellectual application to tasks or exercise – but function on a twenty-four-hour cycle linked to patterns of light and dark that affect secretion of the sleep hormone, melatonin. We are what are termed diurnal mammals, designed to function during daylight hours and sleep at night when it's dark, not nocturnal like some species. But within this diurnal way of functioning there is a degree of variance, thought to be genetically determined, between us, with some people being more naturally inclined to wakefulness in the morning and others later in the day – larks or owls, depending on your chronotype.

The most obvious example of how our biological clock can be affected is when we fly across time zones and suffer jet lag, which occurs when we try to work against our circadian rhythms. The greater the distance, the greater the time difference, and as a consequence, the greater the impact this has on us. And this impact shouldn't be underestimated. Recent research from the University of Stanford in the US, published in 2008, showed evidence that our circadian clock may have a critical impact on memory function. Biologist Norman Ruby's work with Siberian hamsters involved artificially knocking out their circadian clock and seeing how they functioned. Though not renowned for their academic prowess, hamsters are what amounts to being street smart about their environment and, using this criterion, Ruby was able to identify memory deficits.

The change in learning retention as a result of inhibiting the circadian clock appears to hinge on the amount of a neurochemical called GABA (gamma-aminobutyric acid) that is secreted, which acts to regulate and inhibit excitability in the brain. All mammal brains function according to the balance between neurochemicals that excite the brain and those that calm it. The circadian clock controls the daily cycle of sleep and wakefulness by inhibiting different parts of the brain and by releasing, or inhibiting, the secretion of GABA. But if the hippocampus – the part of the brain where memories are stored – is overly inhibited, then those circuits responsible for memory storage don't function properly. 'Those circuits need to be excited to strengthen and encode the memories at a molecular level', says Ruby.

Ruby's findings may also have implications for the decline in memory function that older adults, in general, experience. He explains:

> In ageing humans one of the big things that happens is that the circadian system starts to degrade and break down. When you get older, of course, a lot of things break down, but if the circadian system is a key player in memory function, it might be that the degradation of circadian rhythms in elderly people may contribute to their short-term memory problems. There are a lot of things that could cause memory to fail, but the idea would be that in terms of developing therapeutic treatments, here is a new angle. This is also important because it is one of the first lines of evidence that shows that losing your circadian timing actually does cost you something. It makes it hard to learn things.

Not being able to retain or learn information will inevitably make concentration difficult, so if your lifestyle has little in the way of regularity or daily routine, which can arise not only from travel across time zones but also from keeping very haphazard hours that challenge your circadian rhythms, then you may find this has an impact. Shift workers are particularly susceptible, and it has been documented that a disproportionally high number of accidents occur because of shift work, which may point to significant lapses in concentration. Adolescents, whose sleep needs dramatically increase for a period, and the elderly, whose sleep needs decrease, may find this im-

pact on their biological clock a problem – all of which goes
to show that the sleep/wake cycle is relevant to us all, to a
greater or lesser degree. If you already know that you are
more alert and function better at a specific time of the day,
then choose this time for those tasks that you know require
the most concentration from you (if you don't, see below).
Not only will you accomplish more, but you will also be reinforcing your ability to concentrate, which you can then apply
at other times when you are feeling less alert or are exposed
to greater distractions.

What's your chronotype?

We all have some variance in how we function within the pa-
rameters determined by our circadian rhythms. Some people
are referred to as 'morning people' or larks, because they seem
to find getting up early easier, and like to get going first thing
and then go to bed early. Others consider themselves 'evening
people' or owls, preferring to wake and start the day later, and
more slowly, and only really get going in the early afternoon but
then carry on long into the night. You may think that the time
you wake in the morning is a direct effect of when you went to
sleep and how much sleep you had. For some of us who show
no real morning or evening preference that might be the case.
For others, their inclination may be genetically determined and
will make quite a difference to the choices they would naturally
make about timing of different activities.

Preparation

Whether you are going to sit down to do a piece of work, try
to assemble a complicated piece of equipment or just do some
concentration exercises, how should you prepare? This is
linked to timing. There is no point trying to do something that
requires good concentration skills when the odds are stacked

◈ ARE YOU A LARK OR AN OWL?

The test below will help you identify your chronotype – that is, whether you naturally function better earlier or later in the day.

1. **If you were entirely free to plan your evening and had no commitments the next day, at what time would you choose to go to bed?**
   a) 20.00–21.00   *(5 points)*
   b) 21.00–22.15   *(4)*
   c) 22.15–00.30   *(3)*
   d) 00.30–01.45   *(2)*
   e) 01.45–03.00   *(1)*

2. **You have to do two hours of physically hard work. If you were entirely free to plan your day, in which of the following periods would you choose to do the work?**
   a) 08.00–10.00   *(4)*
   b) 11.00–13.00   *(3)*
   c) 15.00–17.00   *(2)*
   d) 19.00–21.00   *(1)*

3. **For some reason you have gone to bed several hours later than normal, but there is no need to get up at a particular time the next morning. Which of the following is most likely to occur?**
   a) Will wake up at the usual time and not fall
      asleep again   *(4)*
   b) Will wake up at the usual time and doze on
      and off thereafter   *(3)*
   c) Will wake up at the usual time but will fall
      asleep again   *(2)*
   d) Will not wake up until much later than usual   *(1)*

▶

4. **You have to sit a two-hour test, which you know will be mentally exhausting. If you were entirely free to choose, in which of the following periods would you choose to sit the test?**

   a) 08.00–10.00 *(4 points)*

   b) 11.00–13.00 *(3)*

   c) 15.00–17.00 *(2)*

   d) 19.00–21.00 *(1)*

5. **If you had no commitments the next day and were entirely free to plan your own day, what time would you get up?**

   a) 05.00–06.30 *(5)*

   b) 06.30–07.45 *(4)*

   c) 07.45–09.45 *(3)*

   d) 09.45–11.00 *(2)*

   e) 11.00–12.00 *(1)*

6. **A friend suggests that you to join him twice a week at the gym. The best time for him is between 22.00 and 23.00. Bearing nothing else in mind, other than how you normally feel in the evening, how do you think you would perform?**

   a) Very well *(1)*

   b) Reasonably well *(2)*

   c) Poorly *(3)*

   d) Very poorly *(4)*

7. **Do you consider yourself to be a morning person (a lark) or an evening person (an owl)?**

   a) Definitely a morning person *(6)*

   b) More a morning than an evening person *(4)*

   c) More an evening than a morning person *(2)*

   d) Definitely an evening person *(0)*

▶

SCORES

Now add the scores together to get your total and compare your total score with the table below to get an idea of your chronotype:

32–28 points: Definitely a morning person
27–23 points: Moderately a morning person
22–16 points: Neither a morning nor an evening person
15–11 points: Moderately an evening person
10–6 points: Definitely an evening person

(Adapted from 'A Self Assessment Questionnaire to Determine Morningness–Eveningness in Human Circadian Rhythms' by J.A. Horne and O. Ostberg, International Journal of Chronobiology, 1976, Vol. 4, 97–110.)

against you – when you have just done an eighteen-hour work day, or you have a bad cold, or haven't eaten for six hours: this will not help. Indeed, under these circumstances, your chance of success could be impeded to the point where your motivation will be undermined.

Preparation is about more than just avoiding bad timing and you will need to be proactive. Like any athlete who is preparing for a big event, or a footballer preparing for an important match, or a singer about to perform in a concert, warming up to your task increases your chances of success. If your goal is to concentrate better at your job, for instance, you can use the time prior to arriving at work as your preparation time. Rather than crashing into bed late the night before, sleeping fitfully and rushing out of the door in ten minutes flat to arrive at your workplace late, a better start would be to ensure that you get a good night's sleep, allowing enough time to wake and prepare for the day with a good breakfast, and then take some exercise – just walking for twenty minutes is enough – before or on the way to work, all of which will enhance your start to the day.

Actively making 'time out' as a hiatus between home and work creates an excellent space for thinking time. As an immediate consequence, you will have a clearer mind and be able to concentrate better straight away, rather than feeling flustered and out of sorts. Exercise in particular has a significant impact on the brain – and can stimulate neurogenesis (the creation of new brain cells), as research has shown – and helps circulation, so that more oxygenated blood reaches the brain. It also provides a kind of 'breathing space' during which you can think through the tasks of the day ahead, which will help you to better organize your priorities before the day gets going. You can also, if you choose, listen to music while you exercise – but choose something melodic and uplifting, in order to focus your mind positively on the day before you.

Using time before getting to work is one way to prepare. Preparing to concentrate can also include a designated 'warm-up' time. It may be that you use this time to gather facts, read around a subject, make a list of priorities and create the context in which your concentration will occur. Many people use this strategy before settling down to doing a task. Part of your preparation should also be to ensure that you have enough time to focus exclusively on what you are planning to do, and that you will be able to work without interruptions that will dissipate your concentration.

Focus your attention

'I never hit a shot, not even in practice, without having a very sharp in-focus picture in my head', says championship golfer Jack Nicklaus. This is a good description of the purpose of focus, because it shows the benefit of pinpointing all your energy in one direction (just as the sun's rays need to be focused, using a magnifying glass, on a single spot, in order to burn). Focus is similar to concentration, but concentration is what occurs when you consciously focus your attention 100 per cent on what you are aiming to do. It doesn't matter whether you're painting a picture, sawing wood, playing a piece of piano music, performing brain surgery, skiing down a hill or doing a maths puzzle: you will always get a better result if you focus and engage your ability to concentrate.

Focusing – the word 'focus' means 'to direct attention and create clarity' – also enables you to envisage your desired outcome, which can be useful when trying to concentrate on accomplishing a particular activity. Focusing on something in your mind, and visualizing what you need to do to achieve your goal, brings together everything you may need to coordinate it. Like Jack Nicklaus, you have to coordinate what you see with how you move your body within the context of your surroundings with the right amount of force to hit your target, whether this is hitting a ball or writing an essay. Award-winning actress Kate Winslet famously used the word 'gather' as an instruction to herself to gather her thoughts, focus her mind and deliver her Oscar acceptance speech in the face of enormous emotion and excitement. Gathering's not a bad place to start when looking to focus.

The other strategy to use is to be consciously aware of times when you did really concentrate, not necessarily at work, but maybe when you were listening to a piece of music, talking to a friend or doing a tricky crossword puzzle – something in which you were fully engaged. What did that feel like? Anchor that experience in your mind, and make the memory as vibrant and real as you can, so that you can visualize the same sensation at a later date. This is the feeling you are aiming for when you truly concentrate: a sense of being very clearly in the moment, when it feels as if everything is coming together in a good way. Knowing that this is what you are aiming for can help you find it in other situations, especially those where you are trying to concentrate more intensely.

⊚ **READY, STEADY, GO . . .**

Always start your working day (at whatever time is most appropriate for your biological clock if you can) by concentrating on the task you know requires most concentration from you for whatever reason. You should be able to focus on this exclusively for up to ninety minutes, after which you will benefit from a break. Either take an actual break, or take a break from the task to do a variety of less demanding tasks, like making a phone call and having a drink (rehydrating can help refocus your attention) before going back to concentrating on your main task again. Allowing yourself enough time to really engage with what you need to do is important because every time you take some time out from it, it can take the brain up to twenty minutes to do the equivalent of rebooting afterwards. When you have completed all you feel able to do on a task, review what you have done, work out where you will pick up on it again to continue and make a note of the next steps you need to take.

Organize your time

Ever had the feeling that you've got too much to do and too little time to do it in? We all feel like this sometimes, but unless you really have got too much to do – which demands another strategy altogether – you may just be feeling overwhelmed because you don't know where to start and have not developed the essential skills of organizing your time effectively to get all those tasks done. Two things that prevent us from organizing our time effectively are not focusing on one thing at a time and not getting rid of the distractions (internal and external) that we explored in previous chapters.

So, first, turn off your phone/BlackBerry or switch them to silent or answer phone, and then ignore any messages that flash up. Close down your email page on the computer (we'll be discussing email management later). Close down MSN, Facebook, your favourite football club or DIY Tips website, Skype or any other web page with which you distract yourself. One estimate reckoned that office workers are interrupted once every three minutes by an email, phone call or person – which makes it hard to imagine how they ever get any work done. Create a clear space within your workspace to reduce distractions, and make sure you have everything you need to accomplish the job you want to do. Remember that anything that shifts your attention away from what you are trying to achieve will break your concentration, and you will waste time trying to refocus.

Make a list, in order of priority, of what you have to do. With some tasks, there may be some preliminary preparatory work that needs doing first. Once that is out of the way, focus on your main goal and roughly allocate the time needed to do it – this may be half an hour or three hours. The amount of time needn't be 100 per cent accurate, but gives you a rough timescale to work to and will help you plan your day so that you can achieve everything on your 'to do' list.

Emails

Email management requires a special note, as it is one of the most invidious forms of procrastination and man-made distraction we have yet to devise. A study by Hewlett Packard in 2005 found that 62 per cent of British adults were addicted to their email, to the point where they were checking messages during meetings, after working hours and on holiday. Half the workers studied felt a need to respond to emails immediately or within an hour, and one in five people reported being 'happy' to interrupt a business or social gathering to respond to an email or phone message. Tom Stafford, a lecturer in psychology and cognitive science at the University of Sheffield and co-author of the book *Mind Hacks*, believes that the same fundamental learning mechanisms that drive gambling addicts are also at work in email users:

> Both slot machines and email follow something called a 'variable interval reinforcement schedule' which has been established as the way to train in the strongest habits. This means that rather than reward an action every time it is performed, you reward it sometimes, but not in a pre-dictable way. So with email, usually when I check it there is nothing interesting, but every so often there's some-thing wonderful – an invite out or maybe some juicy gossip – and I get a reward.

If this sounds like you, you may want to take a conscious stand against the tyranny of emails and the way they erode your con-centration, because every 'quick check' of your emails that you make could cost you twenty minutes of working time as you try to return to the same level of focus. What was origi-nally designed to make communication faster and easier has become addictive for many of us and created its own blight, as it constantly interrupts our lives. The old saying 'Fire is a good servant but a bad master' could equally apply to emails, so take an active stand and make them work for you rather than ruling your life.

Making sure you keep your email demands under control, unlike one woman whose night-time email activities were docu-mented in the journal *Sleep Medicine* in 2009, is probably wise. The University of Toledo Medical Center in the US reported that a severe insomniac, after taking sleeping tablets, had emailed her friends without any knowledge of having done so. To do this, she had had to turn her computer on, use two sets of user-names and passwords, and send various messages. One read: '!HELP ME P-LEEEEESE.' Another message suggested 'dinner & drinks' and then asked the recipient to 'come TOMORROW

EMAIL-MANAGEMENT TIPS

○ Allocate specific times to answer your emails, but don't ever interrupt another job to do so. If you have an email noise alert on your computer, laptop or BlackBerry, switch it off.

○ Use the 'crossword puzzle rule': if doing a crossword puzzle in the middle of something else would appear rude to your companions, then by the same token, don't read or answer an email.

○ When you do read an email, deal with it immediately – answer, file or delete.

○ Keep business hours for business emails. You may think that by answering emails at midnight you look as though you are working hard, but to others, it may look as if you are incompetent at time management and have no family or social life.

○ Unless you need a reply, put 'FYI only – no answer necessary' at the end of your email and encourage others to do the same.

○ Whenever you get an unsolicited email with information you neither want nor need with an 'unsubscribe' option, unsubscribe.

○ Whenever you get any unsolicited junk or 'phishing' emails, don't answer them (as this confirms an active email address) and trash immediately.

○ Do not send round-robin jokes, warnings about online viruses or the like, as they just clog up email traffic and can be irritating to receive.

AND SORT THIS HELL HOLE Out!'. Doctors described it as a case of 'complex, non-violent cognitive behaviour' – which is one way of putting it!

Relaxation

Develop the good habit of taking short breaks between bouts of intense concentration. Lapses in concentration can occur when you become fatigued, and this is when it's easy to become distracted or to start daydreaming. You should be able to work well for at least a ninety-minute stretch – although if concentrating is something you have struggled with in the past, you may have to build up to this – after which, take a ten-minute break away from task. Use this time to move, stretch, rest your eyes, have a drink (water is fine, although you may want fruit juice, tea or coffee) and walk about a bit. This is time to relax, rather than to make a phone call or deal with another area of work. Then return to the task in hand, review what you've done, and you should find, after about ten minutes, that your concentration has returned to the same level that it was at when you broke off from the task.

Periods of relaxation should be built into a working day. They are important downtime for the brain and the body. Many people use leisure activities to relax, and this can work well, although some activities are more effective at relaxing the body and mind, while also improving its ability to function, than others. Many of us already know this in the abstract – sports activities are good for us – but we may not know precisely why this is so. Mihaly Csikszentmihalyi, professor of psychology and education at the Claremont Graduate University in the US, has made a lifetime's study of how we use our time and what we get out of it. In the early 1970s he devised a research method called the Experience Sampling Method, where people carried a pager and at a series of signalled times, every two hours over the course of a week, had to complete a detailed summary of where they were, what they were doing, who they were with and what they were thinking, and, using a numerical score, rate how motivated and happy they felt, their levels of concentration, their self-esteem and more. A unique series of snapshots taken in this way provided a wealth of detail about daily life and from this research, Professor Csikszentmihalyi formulated the concept of 'flow', which he described as 'being completely involved in an activity for its own sake. The ego falls away. Time flies. Every action, movement, and thought follows inevitably from the previous one, like playing jazz. Your whole being is involved, and you're using your skills to the utmost.'

'Athletes refer to it as "being in the zone", religious mystics as being in "ecstasy", artists and musicians as "aesthetic rapture"', says Csikszentmihalyi. 'Athletes, mystics, and artists all do very different things when they reach flow, yet their descriptions of the experience are remarkably similar.'

Professor Csikszentmihalyi's studies have shown that flow is experienced when we relax, too, but in different ways. Those who played sports and games to relax experienced flow for 44 per cent of the time spent on this activity; those who engaged in a hobby to relax, for 34 per cent of the time; and those who watched television for relaxation for 13 per cent. Interestingly, although watching television provided the least benefit to flow (it is, after all, a passive activity and one in which there is limited engagement), those participating in this study tended to spend around four times longer watching television than in other more positive ways of relaxing. Factoring in specific times to relax with activities that create opportunities for 'flow' can be both a good antidote to a busy working life and will contribute to a better way of functioning when you do have to concentrate closely. You are still relaxing, and benefiting from important downtime, but it's still constructive and beneficial to your other, longer term, goal of learning to concentrate better.

Napping

There is some evidence to suggest that taking short naps – no more than twenty minutes – during the day can help to recharge your concentration. The term 'power nap' was coined by social psychologist and sleep researcher Dr James Maas, professor at Cornell University in the US and author of *Power Sleep*, to describe a short period of sleep that occurs before slow-wave sleep kicks in. Such a nap was found to refresh the brain, making it easier to concentrate again afterwards, while avoiding the sleepy feeling that occurs after deeper, interrupted sleep. One recommendation which may help you harness the benefits of controlled power nap is to drink a cup of coffee, which takes around thirty minutes to have a stimulating effect, and then take a nap. This means that the caffeine effect will awaken and alert you after you have napped.

Conclusion

O **Timing is key when you are working on improving your concentration skills.** There's little point doing this when you are tired, uncomfortable or out of sorts. You'll find it hard to concentrate and end up thinking you can't do it. Some people have more energy in the mornings, others in the late afternoon. Pay attention to your body clock and notice when you feel at your best, and allocate this as the perfect time to begin to master the art of concentration.

O **Preparation is important too.** There's little point in trying to concentrate when you've just finished an exhausting eighteen-hour day in the office or when you're so jet lagged from a recent business trip you'd be hard pushed to say, let alone spell, your own name. Just as world-class athletes and opera singers prepare for a big event, if you have a task you know you need to concentrate fully on, then get a good night's sleep, eat a good breakfast, prepare a quiet workplace without distractions and make sure you have all the tools (reports etc.) you need to get the job done.

○ **Begin to notice the times when you are fully engaged and concentrating on what you are doing or someone else is saying,** and try to remember how that felt when you want to concentrate in the same way again. This is a way of starting to focus your attention and is a skill that, once learned, you can bring to bear whenever you embark on something you really want to concentrate on.

○ **Organize your time.** It's all very well leaving everything to the last minute and thriving under the pressure of a self-generated deadline crisis, but what happens when something unexpected happens that puts you under even more pressure? You won't be concentrating on what you're doing, you'll be panicking about what will happen if you miss that deadline or, worse, you'll finish the job and get it badly wrong. Make time your friend, not your enemy, and build in enough time to get something done, even when the unexpected crops up.

CHAPTER SEVEN
Pay attention!
Children and concentration

I'm feeling a bit downhearted this week. Every single thing
I seem to say to the children, they seem to have forgotten
within nanoseconds. Within 10 minutes of doing a practical
science lesson on electricity (which I thought they'd be
interested in), they couldn't tell me what they'd done... I've
stopped lessons and tried teaching the same idea in a different
way, i.e. playing games, and even going out into the yard to
teach. Nothing is working. They have concentration of zero.

Posted on the *Times Educational Supplement* website, January 2007

Know the feeling? Anyone who has had dealings with a child
or young person will be well aware of this scenario. The
truth is, children are capable of great concentration – as
evidenced by the hours they are happy to spend focused, to the
exclusion of all else, on a computer game, for example – but they
may yet have to learn to harness that ability and apply it elsewhere. In short, while the ability to concentrate is something they
can tap into, they still have to learn concentration skills and how
to apply them to tasks and activities they find less interesting.

As we have seen, the developing brain remains a work in
progress pretty much throughout life, but especially during
childhood, when there is an enormous amount of neurological
connecting and pruning going on. But childhood and adoles-

cence are also times when we expect a lot from our children. From the age of five, if not before, when formal education kicks in, the emphasis is very often on academic achievement to the exclusion of almost everything else. While fashions in childhood education have shifted over the years, partly in response to the work of educational psychologists and neuroscientists alike, the recent emphasis on regular testing, league tables and exam results has made the whole process of schooling much more results orientated than ever before. Parents, who want to see results, may be at fault in this respect too. But this is a time when both the personality and identity of our children are being formed alongside a maturing brain, with myriad other important things to focus on other than schoolwork. Personality development, deciding what our values are, how we want to live our lives, what's important – are all forged now, too.

Suffice to say, then, that for many children their growing up includes a lot of emphasis on fitting in with an academic template that may or may not suit them. That said, if they are given the chance to learn the skills that will support this process, individual outcomes could be managed less stressfully. This is important. Stress in childhood has become a genuine concern, with rates of childhood depression increasing over the last twenty years. This in itself is a block to concentration and the ability to learn – which can lead to frustration, anxiety and behavioural problems. An estimated 10 per cent of 16-to-24-year-olds in the UK suffer from depression, which is alarming; but it also means that 90 per cent are not diagnosed with mental health problems, which suggests that their innate optimism and resilience must be helping them through. We should, as parents and teachers, help children harness these positive qualities, rather than suppress them.

Happiness and concentration

In recent years, research on happiness and resilience has paved the way to a greater understanding of what helps facilitate children's concentration and learning. Self-esteem, often derided as being the hallmark of a 'me' generation, is essential. As psychoanalytic psychotherapist Sue Gerhardt writes in her wonderful book *Why Love Matters*, 'confidence in oneself is surely another way of describing self-esteem. Self-esteem is not just thinking well of oneself in the abstract; it is a capacity to respond to life's challenges.'

So self-esteem is important. The ability to take risks and cope with failure is built on an acquired self-confidence and a conviction that effort is worth as much as outright achievement, and the knowledge that we are valued for who we are, not just what we achieve. We learn these values in early childhood from those around us. They're what make us believe it is worth trying to do something, because without these, and the sense of enquiry and hopefulness that come with them, why bother?

Of course, personalities differ greatly and it is undisputed that the inclination towards happiness is rooted in our genes, as a scientific study published in March 2008 showed. The research, published in the journal *Psychological Science*, was led by Dr Alexander Weiss, of the University of Edinburgh's School of Philosophy, Psychology and Language Sciences, and looked at more than 900 pairs of twins. It found that genes played a significant part in determining how happy we are in life.

Scientists already knew that subjective well-being, or how happy we feel, is linked to personality traits, but until then, nobody had looked at whether personality and subjective well-being had any common genetic origins. Dr Weiss and his colleagues studied 973 pairs of twins using the Five Factor Model (FFM), a questionnaire used by psychologists to assess personality. Some of the twins were identical (and therefore genetically identical) and some were not, so it was possible to compare results between these two groups to see how strongly particular personality traits were likely to be influenced by genes. In the study the researchers were specifically interested in the tendency to worry, the ability to be sociable and levels of conscientiousness – three aspects of personality that are linked to subjective well-being and an overall sense of happiness.

The researchers found that those who did not worry too much, and were sociable and conscientious, tended to be happier, and they suggested that this combination acts as a 'buffer', or a happiness reserve, that helps to shield individuals from depression and increase their resilience during stressful times. And from the comparisons drawn between the two twin groups, identical and not, they found that up to 50 per cent of these traits were, indeed, influenced by genetics.

However, it would be a mistake to assume that those born without the 'cheerful gene' can't achieve happiness. Commenting on the twin study, psychologist Dr Alex Linley, from the Centre for Applied Positive Psychology in the UK (www.cappeu.com), argued that even though other studies supported the genetic argument, it would be wrong for anyone to think that nature had dealt them a fixed hand in terms of happiness:

> What it means is that, rather than a single point, people have a range of possible levels of happiness. And it is perfectly possible to influence this with techniques that are empirically proven to work. Simple things, like listing your strengths and using them in new ways every day, or keeping a journal where you write down, every night, three things that you are grateful for, have been shown to deliver improvements.

While being happy, in itself, is no guarantee of success in life, it does tend to support concentration and good learning outcomes. Research published in 2005 by the University of California Riverside in the US showed that happiness, rather than working hard alone, was the key to success. Happy people were more likely to try new things and challenge themselves, which reinforces positive emotion and leads to success in work, good relationships and even better health: 'There was strong evidence that happiness leads people to be more sociable and more generous, more productive at work, to make more money, and to have stronger immune systems', says Professor Sonja Lyubomirsky, who led the research.

There's no doubt that happier people are more productive, cause less trouble (happy people don't tend to vandalize their environments or alienate their neighbours) and have a healthier life, and this makes it easy to see why the UK government has a vested interest in helping people learn happiness skills – as mooted by the Labour education minister in 2009, Ed Balls, with his 'Time to Talk' initiative for children in the UK.

In an effort to find a way to enable his students to learn happiness skills, teacher Ian Morris collaborated with Dr Nick Baylis, a well-being scientist at Cambridge University in the UK, to devise the Well-Being Programme, which was taught to all Year Ten and Year Eleven students at Wellington College, a prestigious private school, in Berkshire. 'Although we were providing sex and drugs education as part of the PSHE (personal, social and health education) curriculum, we didn't seem to have a philosophy to underpin the teaching and wanted to devise a context that would encourage the kids to think', says Morris.

He and Baylis devised what basically amounts to a ten-point skills programme, which covers looking after the body, relaxing the mind, relationships, living in the present, emotional intelligence, facing challenges and taking control, as well as those skills relevant to technology and the environment. Morris continues:

We only have a 40-minute lesson per fortnight to cover this, but we always start off with two elements, a period of stillness and what could be termed 'counting our blessings'. Then we might look at what the mind needs to function well, or why someone might, for example, resort to drugs to solve a problem and what the alternatives are, or how to end a personal relationship well. And we use a variety of ways to cover topics from role playing to freeze framing – which works particularly well with areas like conflict resolution.

Learning skills that increase happiness and resilience also help enhance powers of concentration: as explored earlier, it's far easier to concentrate if you are not fretting about something you can do little about, and it's easier to concentrate if you are feeling positive and not distracted by negative thoughts. In a climate of test-led learning, where emotional intelligence may be sacrificed in the race for scholastic achievement, there is a strong argument for recognizing and actively promoting this fact.

Certainly it may be that the tide on test-led form of education is beginning to turn. Research published in October 2008 by Professor Michael Shayer of the Department of Education and Professional Studies at the University of London suggests that over-testing is leading to a deterioration of ability among today's 14-year-olds. Researchers at King's College London compared the performance of 800 'bright' 13- and 14-year-olds in tests of higher-order thinking skills with similar tests carried out three decades ago, and discovered that the cognitive skills of today's brightest teenagers were on a par with 12-year-olds given the same tests in 1976.

'Before the project started, I rather expected to find that children would have improved developmentally since 1975', says Shayler. 'But our study allows you to compare, directly, children's performance in 2003 with 1975/6. And, by 2003, children of 11–12 were only performing at the level of the average 8–9-year-old in 1976. Moreover, boys' performance has deteriorated at nearly twice the rate of girls'.' Such findings, he points out, may help to explain why, despite seemingly improving examination results, A-level maths and science teachers often report that their students simply don't know as much as they used to.

How can this deterioration be explained? 'I can only speculate because there is no hard evidence', admits Shayer. 'But I would suggest that the most likely reasons are the lack of experiential play in primary schools, and the growth of a video-game, TV culture. Both take away the kind of hands-on play that enables children to comprehend the world around them.'

Shayer also blames this apparent brainpower slump among children on over-testing. 'The moment you introduce targets, people will find the most economical strategies to achieve them. In the case of education, I'm sure this has had an effect on driving schools away from developing higher levels of understanding.'

Students in the UK studying Shakespeare's *Romeo and Juliet* for their English GCSE exams are no longer required to read the whole play. Indeed, they may never get their hands on the full text but just be given photocopied sheets of a scene they need to study, relying on director Baz Luhrmann's 1996 film to get the whole story. Gaining a pass seems to be the required outcome, not learning to enjoy, appreciate, analyse and reflect on superb writing. Likewise your child may achieve a GCSE A-starred pass in Spanish, but can they speak the language? Maybe we need to get back to focusing on a different outcome for education, one where learning is an enjoyable, lifelong approach to connecting with the world around us, not merely a means to an end.

Language and communication

So what can we do to help our children achieve the sort of ability to concentrate that will enable them to learn happily and successfully? Listening skills are part of this, and this requires an ability to concentrate on what is being said. Undoubtedly, this is a process that starts in babyhood, and one of the first steps parents can take to help to create this ability is to give their child lots of one-to-one attention, which will help them develop the listening skills that is the precursor to the development of good language and communication skills. Language is a building block of intelligence, and spoken language is the end result of lots of learned pre-language communication skills. The work of psychologist Gordon Wells, professor of education at the University of California at Santa Cruz in the US, showed that the children who made most rapid language development were those whose parents were more responsive than others' to their child's attempts to communicate. These parents were more likely to acknowledge and praise these attempts, imitate them, repeat statements back to them, talk about what they were doing as they did it and habitually reinforce their child's efforts. Of course, not everyone finds it easy to talk to a baby or child who isn't yet able to communicate or respond in a verbal way – which may explain the popularity of nursery rhymes and songs, which give parents something to say to their verbally unresponsive offspring – but nevertheless this is important. It will usually be a toddler's parent or primary caregiver who is most attuned to these first attempts to communicate verbally, and who will be able to correctly work out what is being communicated and then reinforce it verbally. Rather than repeating exactly what is said, interpreting it correctly and reinforcing it helps to build language skills in a young child.

To demonstrate the power of this, here is an anecdote from child psychologist Allysa McCabe, professor of psychology at the University of Massachusetts at Lowell in the US, where a young child and his father are talking about a dog:

Child: Lathy.
Dad: Lathy?
Child: No. Lathy.
Dad: Oh, you mean Lassie.
Child: Yeth. Lathie.

The parent, focusing on the object that the child is concentrating on, correctly interprets the name of the dog, at the same time as reinforcing its proper pronunciation, but without inhibiting his child's efforts to communicate and develop his language skills.

What is probably worth a quick mention here is that babies need to hear in order to reproduce speech accurately – hence the routine hearing test babies are given in the UK at birth and at

> ### ◉ QUIET TIMES
>
> For young children, try to include a quiet time at some point in their day when they can learn the importance of taking 'time out' of their busy schedules to recharge. Turn off any background noise, whether this is a radio, TV or computer, and use this quiet time as an opportunity for some peaceful one-to-one communication or completely silent downtime. Helping children achieve this, so that they can use quiet times as a resource for themselves as they get older, is a useful lifelong skill.

around eight months to check that there isn't a physical problem – and this also means that they hear better, focus more easily and concentrate on listening to the spoken word when there is less background noise. Constant TV, radio or music may be fine for adults, but babies need background noise to be kept to a minimum when they are trying to concentrate on listening, in order to hear language sounds distinctly and reproduce them accurately. This is also important in learning to read, as letter recognition – associating a written symbol with a sound – starts aurally. So, recognizing letter sounds, and how they work together, also depends on being able to hear clearly. Being able to hear without distraction is also an adjunct to concentration: it's easier to concentrate fully on one thing at a time, in this case listening, without the distraction of incessant background noise.

The importance of diet

Generally speaking, the smaller an animal, the higher its metabolic rate, which is why mice, for example, have to eat more or less constantly. For such a small organ, the brain demands a lot of fuelling and in fact, it uses about 20–30 per cent of our total energy needs. Nutritious food, eaten at regular intervals, is crucial in childhood to meet these energy needs and support brain development. The brain can only store limited energy at a time, which explains why eating meals regularly throughout the day has been reported to improve brain function. Regular meals allow a constant supply of energy. And perhaps the most important meal of the day for a child is breakfast.

> Skipping breakfast can mean poor energy and concentration levels in the first half of the school day. This can also lead to poor academic performance. Often, children compensate for the lack of breakfast by buying foods like crisps and chocolate, and this encourages bad eating habits.

So says the UK government's own website, www.direct.gov.uk, and this explains why so many schools in the UK now run breakfast clubs – providing breakfast for their children, particularly in designated Education Action Zones to help the estimated 20 per cent of children who never receive breakfast before coming to school. Research-based evidence consistently shows that eating breakfast helps children concentrate better at school, and while giving them a good breakfast means they have more energy, they are also less disruptive, which helps improve academic performance. Not only that, but research published in October 2008 by the UK's Millennium Cohort Study found that children who were obese were twice as likely not to eat breakfast than those of normal weight.

Breakfast is very important because an overnight fast means that blood-sugar levels are low in the morning, and without food, children will feel irritable and tired, which makes it difficult for them to concentrate. Many studies have now shown that children who eat breakfast each morning perform better in school than those who skip the first meal of the day. 'Research has shown that eating breakfast may improve children's problem-solving abilities, their memory, concentration levels, visual perception and creative thinking', says Dr Joanne Lunn, senior nutrition scientist at the British Nutrition Foundation.

'Breakfast is a must, even if your child says he doesn't feel like it', says former teacher, and co-director of the UK's Food and Behaviour Research charity, Dr Alex Richardson, in her book *They Are What You Feed Them*. 'In fact, the very people who "can't face breakfast" are often the sugar-sensitive types who need it most. What can happen is that their blood-sugar levels fall so low during the night that it takes a surge of adrenalin to wake them up at all . . . Then they are usually slow, groggy and grumpy until the adrenalin really starts to kick in.'

So what constitutes a good breakfast for children? Not crisps and sweets washed down by a fizzy drink and eaten in the back of the car on the way to school. Ideally, it should include a combination of carbohydrate and protein, plus some fresh fruit or fruit juice. Eggs, in one form or another, with toast provide both protein and carbohydrate, but there's no reason why you can't have cheese on toast, or toast and peanut butter. Grilled bacon and tomatoes also provide protein and a fresh vegetable (or fruit, to be more accurate). But if a cooked breakfast is too much to manage on a school morning, then breakfast cereals, which should be low-sugar – porridge oats, Ready Brek, cornflakes or Weetabix – plus some fresh fruit such as a sliced banana on top, are also good. Even a toasted bagel with sliced avocado (the routine breakfast of choice for one adolescent girl I know) fits the bill more than adequately. Go for whatever they will eat, whether it's cream cheese on a cinnamon and raisin bagel, peanut butter on a toasted crumpet, hummus on oatcakes or a ham sandwich. If all else fails, resort to making your own banana or carrot cake, or oat and raisin cookies, to offer – but make sure you resist the lure of 'breakfast bars', which are heavy on sugar and low on protein and slow-release carbohydrates. Fruit smoothies can also provide carbohydrate and protein, using natural yogurt rather than milk for increased nutritional benefit as the base, and any fruit – even frozen berries – is good.

Regular drinks are also important, but these should be diluted fruit juice, milk or water, not carbonated drinks, which with their excessive amounts of added sugar are a complete no-no especially at mealtimes. Their high sugar content actually works to diminish any appetite for the sort of slow-release carbohydrates necessary to sustain your child throughout the school day and worse than that, the body has to utilize its precious vitamin B resources, important for cell growth and repair, and the immune and nervous systems, in order to offset all that sugar. Encourage water as a drink, too, rather than always offering juice or milk.

Avoid junk food

Have you ever put petrol into a diesel car engine? Petrol wrecks a diesel engine's lubrication process, and is particularly damaging to its costly, high-pressure pump, fuel injection system and filters; and it can cost up to £6,000 to repair the engine. Which means it's not a mistake you'll make more than once. Similarly, although it can't be a direct comparison, feeding children junk food can have a significant and detrimental effect on their ability to function at school – as TV chef Jamie Oliver showed with his 2007 campaign to improve school meals in the UK. The children's ability to work better in class was significantly improved by their change in diet. So how important is the quality of food we give to children?

A study of 14,000 children in Bristol, published in 2008, showed that even when other factors, such as low income or poor housing, were removed, diet significantly affected the children's development. Those who lived on junk food – foodstuffs like sweets, crisps and chicken nuggets – from an early age were, as a consequence, 10 per cent more likely to be falling behind academically between the ages of six and ten than their classmates. The researchers say that the findings point to the long-term effect that eating poorly could have on school performance.

◈ SNACKS

Children need regular meals, and the four-hour rule (during daytime) is a good one. For a child who has breakfast at 7.00 a.m., but doesn't get lunch until 1.00 p.m., that six-hour gap is too long and they will need a snack in between. Signs of hunger can include extreme grumpiness and non-compliance as their blood-sugar level drops. A snack should, however, be nutritious – a bag of crisps can only be used in an emergency – so opt for a fresh-fruit smoothie, a banana, an oatmeal and raisin cookie (home-made would be good) or some peanut butter on a rice cake. If you are out and about, pop something in your bag, and never take a hungry toddler supermarket shopping unless you actually want a tantrum at the checkout.

Dr Pauline Emmett, a nutritionist from the University of Bristol who worked on the study, said that she was confident that there was a 'robust association' between the children's unhealthy diets and their poor test scores. 'It indicates that early eating patterns have effects that persist over time, so it is very important for children to eat a well-balanced diet from an early age if they are to get the best out of their education.'

Food additives

Another problem with junk food is that it is usually stuffed with food additives, and in particular artificial colourings, which may enhance the look but will do nothing for your child's ability to concentrate. Sodium benzoate (E211), for example, is a food preservative that is both antifungal and antibacterial and can also be used to disguise the taste of poor-quality food. It can also, however, aggravate the symptoms of asthma, particularly when ingested alongside tartrazine (E102), and can even react with vitamin C to form benzene, an aggressive compound known to have carcinogenic properties.

The UK's Food Standards Agency (FSA) has now highlighted a number of artificial food colours – sunset yellow (E110), quinoline yellow (E104), carmoisine (E122), allura red (E129), tartrazine (E102) and ponceau 4R (E124) – that have been linked to a negative effect on children's behaviour. These colours are used in soft drinks, sweets and ice cream, and the FSA recommends that you avoid these if your child shows any evidence of hyperactivity or ADHD. Such is the current level of consumer concern over these additives that in 2008 the UK's Parliamentary Food and Health Forum published a report advocating a legal ban on them, arguing that action is vital to protect children's health. More and more manufacturers are now removing these additives from their products, but it's still worth checking the ingredients list.

Drink more water

Hydration is also important for brain function, and while it's important not to overdo the water intake, most people need to drink more. Water makes up about 80 per cent of the brain and is an essential element in neurological transmissions. Dehydration has been shown to reduce concentration and mental performance, affecting both behaviour and health. A study conducted by consultant paediatrician Dr Trevor Brocklebank at Leeds University in 2002 showed that children's ability to do arithmetic was impaired if they were between 1 and 2 per cent dehydrated – which is not even enough for them to feel thirsty. Symptoms of poor hydration include tiredness, headaches, reduced alertness and less ability to concentrate. Mental performance, including memory, attention and concentration, deteriorates progressively as the degree of dehydration increases.

The UK government recommends that children should drink at least 1.5–2 litres of fluids per day. Obviously, younger children need less. The easiest way of telling whether or not hydration is adequate is to look at the colour of your child's urine. It should be a pale yellow; the darker the colour, the more concentrated it is, indicating inadequate hydration.

Not all fluid intake has to come from water, but caffeinated drinks – cola in particular, as it is notoriously high in sugar – should be avoided. Making sure children get a taste for plain water from an early age is a good idea: offer it first, rather than fruit juices or squashes. Tap water in the UK is safe, so you don't need to rely on expensive bottled water. Filter it first to improve the taste if you like, but don't bother with bottled water, which is no better. In any event, most mineral waters are too high in mineral content for young children, and many are not bacteriologically safe for very young children. Tap water only needs to be boiled (and cooled) first for babies under the age of one year. Sending your child to school each morning with a refillable bottle of water is a good start in encouraging them to drink more, and checking to see how much they've drunk when they get home is also a good idea.

A UK study published in 2008 showed improved outcomes from students at Morecambe Community High School when their water intake level was increased. Students were asked to drink 1.5 litres of water each per day, including weekends, and to complete 'before and after' questionnaires. Their parents and teachers were also asked to complete questionnaires, designed to monitor student concentration levels. Results showed that drinking more water definitely had a positive effect on concentration levels, with 48 per cent of the pupils noticing an improvement. A further 42 per cent noticed a positive improvement in their level of excitability and 38 per cent felt that their anger control had improved. Throughout the trial, several teachers reported that during the afternoon sessions the children were able to stay 'on task' for longer periods of time. The school used the trial in a selection of lessons including statistics, science and maths.

In 2006 the UK's Expert Group on Hydration (EGH) published a report, *Drinking in Schools*, which offers guidance on the importance of adequate hydration for children's health and performance at school. EGH spokesman Dr Paul Stillman says:

> A huge focus has been given to children's nutritional intake – and rightly so. But we are concerned that hydration is at risk of being overlooked as part of that overhaul. Without adequate hydration at school, a child is at risk of experiencing headaches, lack of concentration and digestive problems. This could potentially have a devastating effect on quality of study and performance, as well as adversely effecting health and general well-being.

The *Drinking in Schools* report was based on research carried out at 82 secondary schools in 10 local authorities around the UK. It found that the benefits of hydration for students was recognized, but not seen as a big priority. Ninety-two per cent felt that hydration was a relatively easy problem to solve, yet only 13 per cent were actually trying to solve it with a specific policy on hydration. 'We recommend that children of this age should ideally be drinking two litres of fluid a day, but it looks like many children are not even managing half this amount', said Dr Juliet Gray of the EGH. 'That is bound to take a toll on health, performance and general wellbeing, so we have pulled together some advice on how to improve the current situation.'

The key findings of the report were:

○ Forty per cent of 1- to 18-year-olds were not drinking the FSA's recommended daily minimum amount of 1.2 litres.

○ While at school, children could possibly not have a drink for 8–9 hours a day.

○ Only one school in ten ever gave a child a drink, and few encouraged children to drink throughout the day; even at times when children were most at risk of dehydration (e.g. after physical education lessons), one third of schools offered no encouragement to drink.

○ Only 2 per cent of schools gave children a drink with their lunch and this figure drops to 1 per cent for the morning break.

○ Eighty-three per cent of report respondents knew that pupils would benefit from drinking more fluids throughout the day and 72 per cent believed that better hydration would result in improved classroom behaviour – even while they did little to encourage improved hydration.

○ Two-thirds of schools did not allow any drinking in the classroom, which leaves at least five hours in the day when children were not allowed to drink.

The *Drinking in Schools* report recommended:

○ Every school should have a hydration policy and hydration should be included in plans to review the school meals system.

○ The emphasis of the importance of hydration in the national curriculum needs to be increased.

○ The availability of drinks in schools should be addressed. All schools should provide water fountains and water coolers. Access to fluids at school and, therefore, toilet facilities, should be unrestricted.

○ It would be beneficial to continue to allow children to bring appropriate drinks to school. A blanket ban would be unhelpful and inappropriate.

○ Drinks should be allowed in the classroom and children should be allowed to drink freely during classes. Indeed, they should be encouraged to do so, even if individual schools choose to limit the types of drinks that can be consumed during lessons.

○ If reusable drinks bottles are to be used, care and education need to be exercised with regard to good hygiene practices.

○ Vending machines can provide a controlled choice of drinks to enable adequate hydration. Schools can choose what they stock in these machines and a balance of water, fruit juice, dairy drinks and low-calorie drinks would provide children with access to a variety of beverages that would encourage them to drink frequently.

○ Children should be actively encouraged to drink during morning and lunch breaks.

○ Consideration should also be given to providing an afternoon break.

○ Children should be given active encouragement to drink before, during and after PE and other sporting activities.

Supplements

As stated earlier, supplements should only ever be used to supplement a good diet, not to compensate for a poor one. However, many parents faced with a picky eater will resort to a vitamin supplement or two to make sure their child is getting the key nutrients they need, especially if they are refusing every green vegetable offered. A diverse diet of fresh food, which also ensures the micronutrients needed for absorption, should give your child all that is needed for healthy growth and brain development; but if your child goes through a period of poor eating, then a multivitamin and mineral supplement will probably make you feel happier. Choose one specifically for a child, as the dosage needs to be correct, and from a reputable manufacturer. You tend to get what you pay for with supplements, but you don't need a range of expensive ones either. This isn't nutritional therapy, just supplementation.

ANAEMIA

As with adults, iron-deficiency anaemia is a surprisingly common cause of tiredness, lethargy and consequently – guess what – difficulty in concentration in children. As we have seen, anaemia is a result of low haemoglobin levels, which reduce the red blood cells' capacity for carrying oxygen around the body. Depriving the body's muscles – and brain – of oxygen will make it work less efficiently. Around one in ten children in the UK aged under the age of 4, and almost 50 per cent of girls aged between 11 and 18 years old, have seriously iron-deficient diets, according to the UK's HMSO publication *National Diet and Nutrition Survey*.

Red meat provides the most easily available source of dietary iron, although it can also be sourced from a wide range of vegetables, grains, dried beans and nuts. How much the body actually absorbs depends, partly, on micronutrients – like vitamin C – being available at the same time, which is another good reason for making sure your child eats lots of fresh fruit and vegetables. If your family is vegetarian, you need to pay particular attention to iron intake, and you may wish to include in your menu planning iron-rich tofu, a high-class protein made from soya bean curd that is also suitable for vegans.

If you are worried that your child may be suffering from iron-deficiency anaemia, ask your family doctor for a blood test to check the haemoglobin levels before considering supplementation. Some iron supplements can affect digestion and cause diarrhoea, so opt for a gentler, more bio-available source – and make sure you include more iron-rich foods in your child's diet.

FISH OIL SUPPLEMENTS

One supplement that has actually been marketed to improve children's concentration, and even intelligence, is omega-3 essential fatty acids (EFAs) derived from fish. Although the jury is still out on these marketing claims, other research has suggested positive benefits for children from a diet than includes oily fish.

Cold-water fish like mackerel, herring, tuna, salmon and sardines are an excellent direct source of the omega-3s our brains need, and the current recommendation from the UK's FSA is that adults eat four 140g portions of oily fish every week. If we followed these guidelines, we should get enough omega-3 fatty acids in our diet, but according to some nutritional experts it's not quite as simple as that. You may be eating a diet rich in omega-3 fatty acids but there may be other hidden factors stopping the body from fully utilizing this important nutrient.

There are two key omega-3 EFAs: EPA (eicosapentaenoic acid) and DHA (docosahexaenoic acid). Both can be sourced only from fish. Vegetables provide ALA (alpha lipoic acid), which is an important precursor to EPA and DHA; good sources of this agent include flaxseeds (linseeds) and green vegetables. However, the human body is not good at converting ALA to EPA or DHA, and boys are even less able to make this conversion than girls. In addition, Western diets tend to provide a surfeit of omega-6 EFAs, which compete with omega-3s for absorption, so if you are going to use a supplement, then omega-3 EFAs alone is better than a supplement that also includes omega-6. The most beneficial ratio of omega-6 to omega-3 EFAs is 2:1, while for many this runs at 12:1 or even as high as 20:1, thanks to a general over-availability of omega-6 in our diet.

'Many things can contribute to low omega-3 status', says Dr Alex Richardson, author of *They Are What You Feed Them*. 'One is our high intake of not only omega-6 but hydrogenated and trans fats, found in highly processed junk foods that are high in vegetable fats. These can block the conversion of omega-3s, as will a lack of any one of the co-factors necessary for conversion – vitamin B3 and B6, vitamin C, magnesium, and zinc, to name a few. Stress and some viral infections can inhibit conversion, too.'

When it comes to whether or not children should be given EPA or DHA supplements, it's worth bearing in mind that while DHA supports brain development, EPA supports brain function.

So children from six months to five years benefit from DHA, after which an omega-3 EPA supplement would be the one to choose. And if you are going to supplement, choose one that has enough of the active ingredient in it to be useful: you need to be supplementing at around 400mg of omega-3 a day to make any difference. So if you buy a product with 240mg per capsule, you will need to give two a day. Don't be tempted to buy fish oil capsules where the amount of EPA per capsule is minimal, because you would have to give several capsules a day to get an adequate amount of EPA. This is not only more costly but also means you may end up, inadvertently, giving your child too much vitamin A, which is also present in fish oil and which may be harmful in excess. It may mean choosing a more expensive product to get an adequate amount of active ingredient, the EPA, but it would probably work out more cost-efficiently in the long run.

EPA is also effective in the treatment of depression, as demonstrated by a double-blind, randomized trial from the Tehran University of Medical Sciences, published in March 2008 by the *Australian and New Zealand Journal of Psychiatry*. It showed that 1g a day of EPA and 20mg a day of fluoxetine (commonly known as Prozac) had equal therapeutic effects when used by patients with clinically diagnosed depression – making it a possible alternative for the treatment of depressed children, for whom SSRI antidepressants like Prozac aren't recommended.

Sleep

It's really very simple: a tired child will find it difficult to concentrate. A chronically overtired child will find it difficult to manage life at all, let alone concentrate, and a high proportion of behavioural problems in young children can be directly attributable to lack of sleep. Many children, of all ages, get less sleep than they need. If you want to know what this feels like, remember how you felt after an air journey across several time zones and how difficult jet lag made it to concentrate? Some children suffer similar effects from chronic tiredness. Babies need a lot of sleep, and adolescents need almost as much: both infants and teenagers often have poorly regulated body clocks. Tired children will find daily life tricky solely because they are tired, and that includes trying to function at school and concentrate on schoolwork.

Ideally, a 1-year-old-baby should still be sleeping around 12–14 hours out of 24, with a healthy sleep pattern of 10 hours at night, topped up by a couple of daytime naps. A 5-year-old still needs around 11 hours' sleep, and since daytime naps will have become a thing of the past, this will be at night-time. Aged 10, a child still needs 10 hours a night and even at 15, 9 hours a night will significantly help improve daytime performance. Chances are, though, that your adolescent is getting to bed at around 11.00 p.m., and then waking with difficulty at 7.00 a.m. during the school week. No wonder weekends are spent catching up, but with lots of long lie-ins and daytime sleep, which only serve to throw the all-important sleep/wake pattern into further disarray. The upshot of sleep deprivation, at any age, will be a permanent feeling of jet lag, with all its associated impact on mood, performance and ability. What's more, the sleep your child is getting may not be of good quality, which will further compound concentration problems during the day.

There's no way round this one. If you want your children to be happy, alert and perform well – at whatever age – they need to have enough sleep. If necessary, try introducing an improved bedtime routine (if your children are teenagers, you will need to be subtle about this). Make sure, for example, that you serve your evening meal several hours before bedtime, that homework is done early enough to avoid late-night crises, that you build in enough time for relaxing before bed (a bath, some quiet reading), that you offer a sleep-inducing carbohydrate snack before bed and that you ensure they are sleeping a quiet, dark bedroom. Don't underestimate the effectiveness of a dark bedroom, as melatonin (the sleep-inducing hormone that is produced by the pineal gland in the brain) is made only in response to the absence of light. Melatonin helps regulate your child's sleep/wake cycle, so try to avoid leaving a night light on, as this can interfere with this process. If you need to reset your child's sleep pattern, try bringing bedtime forward a little every night – even if it's only five minutes at a time – so that you can help to ensure that they get the sleep they need. Tedious though this rigmarole sounds, you will be rewarded – in time – by a well-rested child who wakes up happy and who is, generally, more amenable because they are not chronically overtired.

Tiredness affects children differently from adults and, paradoxically, an overtired child may become more energetic, hyperactive and speedy as a result of sleep deprivation. Don't misinterpret such behaviour as a sign that this is a child who needs less than average sleep; often those children whose behaviour seems to suggest that they need less sleep than other children are simply compensating for overtiredness. This is because chronic tiredness overstimulates our 'wide-awake' hormones – cortisol and adrenalin – to compensate. These are also stress hormones, so you will get a child who behaves in a stressed fashion: moody, unpredictable, even hyperactive. Adequate sleep goes a long way to helping your child manage life and perform better.

Exercise

We all know that exercise is good for us but what is becoming increasingly relevant is just how important regular exercise is for our intellectual functioning and, in particular, the ability of our children to focus and perform well.

'I cannot over-estimate how important regular exercise is in improving the function of the brain', says John Ratey, clinical associate professor of psychiatry at Harvard in the US, in his 2008 book *Spark: The Revolutionary New Science of Exercise and the Brain*. He argues that physical fitness for students is not only crucial for avoiding obesity but also helps improve academic performance. 'Exercise stimulates our grey matter to produce Miracle-Gro for the brain.'

This 'Miracle-Gro' he is referring to has nothing to do with pot plants but is a brain chemical called brain-derived neurotropic factor, or BDNF. When we exercise, our working muscles send chemicals into our bloodstream, including a protein known as IGF-1. Once in the brain, IGF-1 stimulates the production of more BDNF, and this helps new neurons and their connections grow. In addition, levels of other neurotransmitters are increased after a strenuous exercise session. 'Dopamine, serotonin, norepinephrine – all of these are elevated after exercise', says Ratey. 'So having a workout will help improve focus, help keep you calm and reduce impulsivity.' He goes as far as to describe the effect of exercise as being like a natural dose of Prozac or Ritalin, but without the deleterious chemical side effects.

There is no doubt that regular exercise helps children in a number of very definite ways, including these:

○ Exercise raises endorphin levels, so children feel better about themselves.
○ Exercise will help your child feel less stressed.
○ A child who takes regular exercise will concentrate better when in class.
○ Children who do regular physical activity sleep better at night.

In addition to the benefits listed above, exercise will help release muscular tension which, if left unaddressed, can create feelings of psychological tension, stress and agitation. In children, the body/mind connection is more easily expressed, not least because they are less inhibited than adults, so if they feel bad they will let you know about it. The fact is that the more relaxed a child is, post-exercise, the easier they will find it to concentrate. We are designed for movement, and our bodies benefit greatly from it and, by extension, our minds; but without the opportunities to exercise, we can become physically tense, un-comfortable and easily distracted. People talk about being 'in tune with their bodies' and this is very apparent in children who have the benefit of exercising their bodies regularly and who, as a result, appear more relaxed in them.

A child's inability to sit still, ignore distractions, listen and concentrate constantly frustrates both parents and teachers. Those who subscribe to the theories of neuro-developmental delay believe that there is evidence that this is caused when primitive baby reflexes have not been unlearned and replaced by the more mature reflexes that allow for normal neuro-developmental progress, so mastering the physical and mental skills necessary for, say, reading and writing becomes delayed. This is seen most dramatically in children with developmental coordination disorder, or dyspraxia, and can also be related to autistic spectrum disorders. However, it is thought that these conditions are the extremes of the symptoms that delayed neuro-development can cause. Exercise that takes a child physically back to the baby reflex stage and replaces this with more mature reflex movements can help, and there are now special programmes of specific exercises that have been designed to achieve this.

These exercises, sometimes referred to as 'sensory integration therapies', are based on principles developed by therapists attached to organizations in the UK such as the Developmental Practitioners Association and the Institute for Neuro-Physiological Psychology (INPP) in Chester, and they allow children to progress through the important physical developmental stages needed for the body and brain to prepare for learning. The exercises are usually done daily, in short bursts of ten to fifteen minutes, and involve simple repetitive movements such as rocking, crawling, jogging on the spot, windmill arms, slithering, pulling with arms and legs and standing stiff like a robot. To make them more enjoyable, the exercises can be accompanied by rhymes, rhythms and music.

This therapy was the thinking behind the work of Joy High, an occupational therapist based in the UK, who worked with teachers at a local primary school, Bentley West in Walsall, to devise a ten-minute exercise programme for Year Four (8- to 9-year-olds) children who were not doing well at school. Dubbed 'The Cool Kids' programme, it was based on the principles of sensory integration therapy and devised to allow children to go through the normal stages of physical development.

The Cool Kids programme of exercise, now running at seventeen different primary schools in the Wolverhampton area, involves children lying on their fronts and backs on the floor, rolling on their fronts and backs and working their way up towards four-point kneeling; crawling on hands and knees, leading up to standing; and once standing, activities such as skipping. The activities are done in a group, with each individual child taking a turn, and it is recommended that teachers run the twelve-week course at their own pace, as some children may take longer to get through the programme than others. Many of the schools now using it run the programme at the beginning of the day for ten minutes, enabling the children to prepare for their learning, and all those participating confirm that the three main outcomes from introducing the Cool Kids programme are an improvement in concentration, improvement in behaviour and, unsurprisingly, children being more teachable.

The INPP has also developed a short ten-minute exercise programme for use in all schools. UK studies in both Cumbria and Derbyshire have found that the programme is twice as effective as traditional exercise and four times better than no physical activity at all in improving reading, writing and behaviour in primary schoolchildren. A study of 670 children, with an average age of 8, in seven schools in Northern Ireland showed improved concentration and a trend towards higher academic achievements. As a result, Northumberland County Council has now trained some seventy-five classroom assistants to use the exercise programme in the county's primary schools, as part of their behaviour support service.

A simple example that illustrates the theory is that being able to stand on one leg successfully turns out to be intrinsically linked to reading ability. 'It may sound far fetched, but the science is well established', says psychologist Sally Goddard Blythe, director of the INPP and author of *Attention, Balance and Coordination: The ABC of Learning Success.*

While these specific exercise programmes benefit concentration and learning, ordinary regular activity every day – whether in the form of formal or informal exercise – is beneficial too. The current UK government guideline for exercise for children is one hour of physical activity every day, although this recommendation stems from a focus on reducing obesity rates rather than improving intellectual performance. Unless a child is already getting a regular amount of physical activity a day – the sixty-minute guideline is just that, a guideline, and any regular exercise is better than none – lack of exercise may already be making a noticeable impact on their ability to concentrate, whether a toddler or a teen. Suffice to say, then, that if you feel your child's academic progress could benefit (as well as their physical fitness), it's well worth introducing regular exercise and physical activities. Even better, find activities that all the family can enjoy, which will not only enable you and your child to spend quality time together: any exercise you do together will benefit you too!

At present in the UK, there is such an emphasis on reducing obesity and generally improving the nation's health that local opportunities for activity have been greatly improved, from local authority classes to clubs. There's no time like the present for you and your family to benefit: check them out.

Yoga

One form of exercise that has become increasingly popular with children, from toddlers to teens, in recent years is yoga. The many benefits of yoga – increased flexibility and strength, joint mobility, posture – include the benefits to concentration, partly because of yoga's emphasis on creating and holding a posture, while coordinating breathing. Concentrating on getting your body into a certain position, holding it and moving on to another posture means you have to focus exclusively on what you're doing, which can help create the habit of concentrating on one thing at a time – a useful discipline in itself in the frenetic, multitasking lives to which children are increasingly exposed. Learning the additional skill of breath control and matching the breath to the movement also helps improve concentration and focus.

Meditation

'The problem is stress', says William Stixrud, PhD, a clinical neuropsychologist from Maryland in the US. He specializes in work with children and adolescents, and has studied and lectured frequently on the effects of stress on the brain, particularly its effect on the developing brain.

> Not only does stress interfere with functions such as attention, memory, organisation, and integration, but prolonged stress actually kills brain cells and shrinks the brain's main memory structures. In fact, the top stress researchers in the world report that a lifelong high stress level is the best predictor of risk for Alzheimer's disease and other forms of dementia. In light of this research, I am increasingly struck by how counterproductive it is for students to learn in highly stressful contexts, since stress not only interferes with their learning and retention in the short run, but also burns out their brains in the long run.

The answer, Dr Stixrud says, is meditation – and in particular Transcendental Meditation® or TM®, which 50,000 students in the US have been taught in a programme funded by the David

Lynch Foundation (set up by film maker David Lynch, who has meditated for thirty years, to provide funds for children in the US who want to learn to meditate). 'I have been a big fan of using meditation in schools for many years due, in part, to its unparalleled ability to create the experience of relaxed alertness in students – and to create learning environments in which students feel safe to tackle very difficult material and assignments', says Stixrud.

The David Lynch Foundation's Quiet Time/Transcendental Meditation® programme is practised by students twice a day at school, at the beginning and end of the school day, and those participating have been shown to quickly benefit from better levels of concentration, increased creativity and academic achievement, while, at the same time, levels of anxiety and depression are reduced, as are sleep and eating disorders, and symptoms of ADHD and other learning disorders.

In the UK, the Maharishi School in Lancashire caters for children from aged 4 to 16, and practises meditation twice a day. The school has an excellent record of academic achievement and GCSE results that are far better than national average. Derek Cassells, the headteacher, thinks meditation is the key and, interestingly, he regards stress as the underlying cause of all learning and behavioural problems:

> We have a very traditional curriculum. But, because we also have TM® or word-of-wisdom for the younger children, they experience a level of rest that is at least twice as deep as deep sleep, twice every day. Stresses and tensions are released and the nervous system is brought into balance. From that balance come all the benefits – such as a greater ability to focus and concentrate – and this produces good academic results. These aren't our goal; they're just a side effect. What's important is that the children are so at ease, they automatically enjoy learning and they can utilise more of their potential. We just bring out what's already there.

Other schools in the UK are introducing similar 'quiet times' or meditation periods. St James Independent School in west London encourages not only twice-daily meditation but also a 'pause' at the beginning of each activity, to allow time to focus before embarking on the next activity. David Fontana and Ingrid Slack, co-authors of *Teaching Meditation to Children*, are psychologists who specialize in working with children. They too believe that children should be taught to meditate because it gives even very young children power over their thinking and their emotions, not by a repressive self-control but by enhanced self-understanding and self-acceptance. Fontana and Slack advocate meditation as a gentle and effective means of overcoming a wide variety of psychological and behavioural problems, such as anxiety, hyperactivity and aggression, and they back this up with case histories.

Developmental Coordination Disorder (DCD) – dyspraxia

You may wonder if your fidgety, clumsy child who cannot remember anything for longer than two seconds has more of a problem with concentration than is considered normal. Is this just a case of intermittent 'ants in his pants', or is he suffering from some degree of dyspraxia? An estimated 6 per cent of the UK population is thought to be affected, with boys twice as likely to be affected as girls. It could be worth ruling dyspraxia out but it may also be worth trying some of the measures outlined above first, before you embark on what can sometimes be a lengthy process of educational assessment that could inadvertently make your child anxious. However, if dyspraxia is the cause, then the good news is there is a lot that can be done to improve things.

In the UK, the first step is to ask for an assessment, which can be done by an educational psychologist, an occupational therapist or a physiotherapist with special training. Julia Dyer, a physiotherapist who runs a practice for children in Lancashire, in the UK (www.juliadyer.com), outlines those problems a child might have that could signify DCD (but do keep in mind, as you read this list, that there may be age-appropriate delay or other reasons for difficulties):

O poor concentration and easily distracted
O unable to remember and follow instructions
O poorly organized
O problems sitting still or always on the move
O difficulty with handwriting or using scissors
O problems with getting dressed or learning to tie shoelaces
O difficulty copying from a book or blackboard
O problems with maths and writing stories
O difficulty making and keeping friends
O slow to reach milestones such as sitting, crawling, walking and speaking
O poor motor skills compared to their peers, e.g. running, hopping, catching a ball
O falls over frequently or bumps into objects
O difficulty riding a bicycle
O dislikes PE and games
O messy eater or struggles to use a knife and fork together
O dislikes some sensations such as loud noises, labels in clothing, messy play, hair washing and cutting.

Although there is no cure for dyspraxia, learning how to manage its impact can make all the difference to a child's ability to concentrate and make the most of his or her learning opportunities. Diet, exercise, adequate sleep and specific measures designed to enable a child to reach his or her potential can be explored.

ADHD spectrum

Attention deficit hyperactivity disorder, commonly abbreviated to ADHD, is generally considered to be evident in a child who meets various criteria linked to having a problem with impulsivity and inattention, with or without hyperactivity.

The spectrum, or range, of ADHD and its impact can vary hugely but it is thought to affect between 3 and 5 per cent of children (again, boys are affected more often than girls) and it is usually diagnosed before the age of 7.

The three main aspects of ADHD are classified by a variety of behavioural problems, and may also be linked to anxiety or depression. Inattention is characterized by being easily distracted, having difficulty in listening, a tendency to zone out or daydream and being unable to finish off one activity before starting another. Impulsivity is characterized by acting without thought, jumping from one activity to another, finding it impossible to take turns and so constantly interrupting other people's conversations, and being generally disorganized. Hyperactivity is characterized by perpetual restlessness, inability to sit still, constant fidgeting and restless sleep at night.

Because it is quite normal for all children to experience some aspects of this type of behaviour from time to time, it's important to look at other reasons for behavioural problems – from chronic overtiredness, to food additives, to boredom – before unnecessarily pathologizing normal behaviour, or assuming that is the child definitely has ADHD. If you think there is a problem, however, getting a professional opinion or diagnosis from a child specialist is imperative, while bearing in mind that there may be a lot you can do to help your child manage whatever is the root cause of their difficult behaviour and poor concentration skills.

Steve Biddulph, author of the wonderful book *The Secret of Happy Children*, tells the story of a man whose 8-year-old son was diagnosed with ADHD and the recommendation was that he be prescribed Ritalin. The father wasn't sure what ADHD meant, but took it at face value and concluded that his son wasn't getting enough attention. So he, a truck driver who worked long hours, changed his working schedule to spend more time with his son. He was around more after school, during the school holidays and spent time with him at weekends.

Within six months, the boy was off Ritalin and no longer had a diagnosis of ADHD. What this anecdote shows is that sometimes challenging behaviour is not all it seems.

TV, computer use and video games

The one occasion when you can virtually guarantee seeing concrete evidence of your child's ability to concentrate is when they are caught up in a television programme, instant messaging their friends or participating online in a particularly ruthless-looking war game. Inevitably, though, our concern about this sort of concentration is about its context and the content of the activity. How much TV should we let our children watch? Are video games bad for them? When was the last time you heard a parent complain that their child spent too much time reading books? This was a concern of Greek philosopher Plato back around 400 BC, when he lamented that reading would be the downfall of the oral tradition and memory (turns out he was probably right!). There is no holding back progress, as they say, but every generation judges it differently – and the generation gap is very much alive and well, especially when it comes to the use of information technology, or IT.

Time was when parents routinely worried about their children watching too much television – today, we'd be quite glad if they were watching a wholesome mix of child-oriented news, activity and information like the BBC's *Blue Peter*, as children did in the 1970s – but as was ever the case, children tended to watch it if they had nothing better to do. Now, most children from the age of 5 up are computer savvy, and they may well opt for using the computer to play, communicate or (occasionally) study, before checking out what's on the TV. Today, 82 per cent of children aged 7 to 17 use the internet, according to the 2008 Pew Internet and American Life Project report on Networked Families, and while internet use has increased, TV watching has declined. And if there is some cult TV programme, they'll watch it in their rooms while instant messaging their friends, who may also be watching at the same time in their own homes. In other words, watching television is no longer the social family activity it once was.

In their book *Consumer Kids*, published in 2009, Ed Mayo, CEO of Consumer Focus (a campaigning charity for the consumer, www.consumerfocus.org.uk), and academic Dr Agnes Nairn PhD, professor of marketing at EM-Lyon Business School in France and RSM Eramus University in the Netherlands, who specializes in marketing and children, included research that showed that children's bedrooms in the UK have become high-tech media bedsits. Ninety per cent of teenagers have a TV in their bedrooms, as do 60 per cent of 5- to 6-year-olds. The trend is for 98 per cent of teenagers from deprived backgrounds having a set in their room, compared to 48 per cent from more affluent homes. Two-thirds of 5- and 6-year-olds watch TV before school in the morning. More than a third of children have their own laptop or PC, and two-thirds own a games console. On average, British children spend five hours and eighteen minutes watching TV, playing computer games or going online *every single day*. Over a year, this adds up to 2,000 hours, compared to 900 hours spent in class and 1,270 hours spent with their parents, according to *Consumer Kids*.

The problem with this is that, if you are spending five hours a day online, watching TV or gaming, you can't be spending that time on the schoolwork that might improve your academic outcome – there just isn't enough time in the day. And, as we saw in Chapter One, it's spending time on something that produces results. In 2009, at just 14 years old, Dan Searjeant achieved a 100 per cent in his Grade Eight saxophone exam, after playing the instrument for only four years. Although musically gifted, he's not a genius, but he enjoyed playing so much that he practised for three hours a day, and that's what made the difference. 'It used to be a hobby but in the last two or three years I've got into it much more', he said. 'The turning point came when I spoke to another saxophone student who was really good but said he wished he'd practised more when he was a teenager. I didn't want to reach twenty and regret I hadn't done it.' It occurs to me I have yet to meet anyone who has said they wished they'd spent more time as a teenager playing *Grand Theft Auto*.

Today's children and young adults have been dubbed 'digital natives' by Dr Gary Small, Director of the UCLA Memory and Research Centre at the Semel Institute for Neuroscience and Human Behaviour, and author of *iBrain: Surviving the Technological Alteration of the Modern Mind*. They have always had access to computers, the internet and online games: these form the backdrop to their lives. The task of their exasperated parents and teachers is to work with this, and find some way to utilize the concentration skills they have honed at the flat screen and make them applicable across a wider spectrum of activity.

So, are computer games bad for children?

In 2006, Dr Simon Bradford from the UK's Brunel University published the results of a three-year study that addressed the issue of whether computer games were bad for children, given that they were spending as much time online playing as they were doing their homework. What researchers found was that gaming was a far from antisocial activity.

The focus of the study at Brunel University was a free-to-access, online gaming world called *RuneScape*, similar to the American games *Warcraft* and *Everquest*, which focuses on role play, where the emphasis is on character development. *RuneScape* provides gamers with an arena in which they can play with identity and act out experiences that may be impossible in the material world – and, the researchers suggested, potentially offering young people the chance to develop important social and cultural skills, which carry significance for real life.

The researchers went on to emphasize that gaming can provide teenagers with access to a complex world where problem solving is key. So, they concluded, those who view teenage gamers with disdain and concern might find themselves surprised to see youngsters who are actually very socially accomplished. The complexity and structure of most games means that teenage gamers are actually learning some vital skills – including concentration – which will stand them in good stead as they prepare for the labour market. The problems can arise when teenagers are spending time gaming to the exclusion of all else.

Multitasking, or just muddling through?

When it comes to TV and gaming it would seem they are good servants but bad masters – and when it comes to children utilizing the benefits of what's on offer, balance is key. Playing games to the exclusion of all else is obviously detrimental to a young person's other skills or physical fitness, but playing games does have a value, not least in that it provides a social currency on which many young people build their relationships. What is of growing concern, however, is the penchant for children and young people to multitask – to constantly do a variety of things at the same time – and this can have a negative effect on their ability to concentrate on one thing at a time, with detrimental outcomes.

Maybe it's a scene you're familiar with. Checking in on your teenager in her room, where she is supposed to be writing a homework essay or revising for a test, you find her with a school book on her lap, instant messaging her friends, with music blaring from her iPod and the TV on. 'It's OK,' she tells you, waving the schoolbook in your face – 'I *am* revising.' Unsurprisingly her score on the test is a poor pass, when you know she's capable of doing better. 'It's OK,' she says again, 'I *passed*!' While we can applaud their digital efficiency, and their social competence – after all, she has 316 'friends' on Facebook – somehow you know that all this ceaseless connectivity isn't serving her well. And you're right.

Continuous Partial Attention, or CPA, is a term first coined in 1998 by software executive Linda Stone, when she noticed the prevailing trend to use information technology to do several things. Children and young people, who are particularly at home with IT – indeed, in the UK, it's a compulsory part of the school curriculum from primary school upwards – have become adept at juggling several things at once: learning a few French verbs while waiting for something to download or a friend to respond via the MySpace chat room. It's become a habit to dip in and out of something, never wholly focusing on one thing at a time. And this ability may come at a price, for as the adolescent brain adapts to this way of doing things, it becomes increasingly difficult to ever 'switch off'. 'People lose the skill and the will to maintain concentration, and they get mental antsyness', says David Meyer, director of the Brain, Cognition and Action Laboratory at the University of Michigan in the US, describing the sort of mental fidgetiness and attention deficit that makes it difficult to concentrate on one thing at a time. 'The toll in terms of slowdown is extremely large – amazingly so', Meyer continues. 'If a teenager is trying to have a conversation on an email chat line, while doing algebra, she'll suffer a decrease in efficiency, compared to if she just thought about algebra until she was done. People may think otherwise, but it's a myth.'

This sort of multitasking is quite taxing to the brain, which is designed to process information sequentially rather than all at once, and requires the input of various stress hormones like norepinephrine and cortisol to support these extra demands. This in turn creates a constant state of alertness, which is why it becomes difficult to switch off, and this state starts to feel normal. Once it feels normal, the inclination is to maintain it, seeking out the circumstances that keep those hormones churning. While this is not a true addiction, it's a habit that young people find hard – and have no inclination – to break. It's also worth remembering that an excess of cortisol, which binds more easily to neuro-receptor sites than dopamine or serotonin, reduces input of calm and happy feelings, creating the sort of anxious feelings that make concentration difficult.

Instilling good habits as soon as your child becomes IT savvy is a good idea. Introduce the idea of concentrating on one thing at a time, getting the maths homework out of the way before talking to friends online while watching TV, for example. Not only does the maths homework get done quicker, but the process of doing it is more easily learned and reapplied in the future when that same information needs to be retrieved for a test or exam. Your child doesn't have to work harder, but is working smarter, to get a better outcome. Make working smart your child's aim, and create good learning habits that both enable concentration and benefit from it.

It's also worth remembering that all this cyber-communicating denies children the time for real-life personal relationships. Being able to manage personal relationships involves developing emotional intelligence and this is going to be difficult to achieve without spending time with other people. Research shows that 55 per cent of communication is conveyed by the body language we use – that is, use of eye contact, gestures and facial expressions – while 38 per cent is conveyed in the voice – its quality, use of tone and inflections – and only 7 per cent is conveyed in the words we use. Children may be communicating as never before, but they are not doing it in person, so learning how to read non-verbal communication cues will be difficult.

Boost your child's concentration – checklist

If you are now inspired to take positive steps towards improving your child's concentration, have a look at the suggestions below.

ROUTINE
Unfashionable though it is, routine is a way of establishing fixed but flexible points in the day that allows children the opportunity to get on with what they need to do to grow and develop

and concentrate, without having to worry about what's happening next. Lack of routine can be very distracting and also create insecurities around daily events. If you know that you will be woken in time to have breakfast, will be helped to get to school on time, will have food provided regularly so that you are never hungry and will get enough sleep so that you aren't overtired during the day, then you can relax and concentrate on learning. None of this is conscious, but with a routine, there is a sense of security about life. Routine suits most children, whether they are toddlers or teens – although obviously as they grow, their practical and social needs change – so it's worth thinking about how their daily routine supports them.

BREAKFAST

'The body's natural reaction to low blood sugar is to compensate by increasing adrenalin output', says psychologist and director of the Institute for Neuro-Physiological Psychology (INPP) Sally Goddard Blythe. 'Such a biochemical combination can affect attention, concentration and impulse control. In the long term, sharp swings in blood sugar levels increase irritability, fatigue and bouts of hyperactivity.' Even if you now have to reorganize your mornings and take a more creative approach to make sure your children get a breakfast that will help them to stayed focused and concentrate on their lessons, you will be doing them the biggest favour of all, and one that will pay dividends in the long term: breakfast really is that important.

TIME

It takes time to do something well, whether that's making a Lego castle or a cake. Encourage your children to take time over what they are doing – time to become absorbed and engaged in their task and to actually develop the ability to concentrate. By focusing on the activity, rather than the outcome (and getting it finished in the shortest possible time), you can work towards extending their concentration on one thing.

LEARN A SKILL

Learning a musical instrument – even a recorder – helps develop concentration and encourages a focused commitment to the task, as do other more physical activities such as ice skating or skateboarding. It's also an opportunity to learn that doing something well takes time and application, even if your child just wants to bend it like Beckham. Being able to do something well – through application and practice – also enhances self-esteem.

BALANCE

Being online, playing computer games and watching TV are all part of children's everyday culture and do have some benefits, but if they are spending more than two hours a day doing this to the exclusion of real-life relationships, with their family and friends, and other activities, they will be losing out on other positive experiences and key skills.

ALLOW FOR DOWNTIME

Research has shown that the relationship between stimulation and performance forms a bell curve: while stimulation (whether it's caffeine or loud music) can boost performance, too much stimulation is stressful and causes a decline. In addition, the brain needs downtime to consolidate thoughts and memories. Children and teenagers who never have a quiet moment between waking and bed may not get the downtime they need and may find that their brains are constantly on 'red alert', making it difficult for them to focus on one thing, like reading a book, even when they want to. Encourage time out just to chill.

DO THINGS TOGETHER

For young children and teenagers alike, doing activities together gives you the opportunity to work with them, maintaining an interest in what you are doing together and extending their concentration span. Also it gives some much needed time just to be together, working at their pace.

KILL BACKGROUND DISTRACTIONS

Although some background music can help block out other distractions, encourage the ability to work without a musical accompaniment while children are learning to concentrate. When doing schoolwork, for example, ensure that for the period of time it takes, everything else is switched off. This may be tricky if the task itself needs access to a computer, which means that Facebook or instant messaging can be easily accessed, so cajole, reward or even bribe to create the habit of getting work out of the way first.

For some children, who appear to find background noise overstimulating, a quiet environment is especially important. Learning to focus and concentrate in a quiet environment also helps develop a lifelong skill that can then be used in a noisier environment without detrimental effect.

Conclusion

○ **The developing brain is a work in progress throughout life, but never more so than in childhood,** when experiences shape how we think of ourselves and our abilities – including the ability to concentrate. A happy child will learn to focus and concentrate better than one stressed out by endless results-orientated tests, so give your child plenty of downtime.

○ **A bored child or a teenager who cannot see the point of a task will not be able to concentrate.** Think creatively to find ways to get your child engaged in an activity; the greater their engagement, the greater their powers of concentration and the better their learning potential and outcomes.

○ **If you're expecting your child to concentrate through the long school day, make sure you give them a good breakfast.** Research shows, time and again, that eating a healthy breakfast not only helps children concentrate better at school but also makes them less disruptive, which in turn improves academic performance.

○ **Make sure your children drink enough water.** Water makes up about 80 per cent of the brain and is an essential element in neurological transmissions. Dehydration has been shown to reduce concentration and mental performance, affecting both behaviour and health; and in tests, children who were only marginally dehydrated (that is, not even enough to feel thirsty) did less well in maths than those who were drinking plenty of fluids.

○ **Insist your child gets a good night's sleep.** A tired child cannot concentrate. Physical exercise is important too and will also ensure that children sleep, so make exercise fun and age appropriate. Even better, join in yourself for all the same benefits, including better concentration skills.

○ **Put the brakes on multitasking.** Your teen may think they can listen to music, MSN their friends, watch TV, text a mate back and revise for their exams, all at the same time, and argue that it must work because all their friends do it, but they're wrong. Doing anything in a half-hearted way, especially with half a dozen serious distractions, impedes concentration to such an extent they will have no long-term recall of what it is they have been revising. In other words, they will have been wasting their time.

CHAPTER EIGHT

Techniques to improve your concentration

If you could just stay focused on the right things,
your life would stop feeling like a reaction to stuff that
happens to you and become something that you create:
not a series of accidents, but a work of art.

Winifred Gallagher

You may think that something as apparently intangible as improving your ability to concentrate won't make very much difference to your life. You can see how, in a practical way, you'd possibly get more done if you were more focused, but can it really make a difference? The amazingly good news is that because of the brain's neuroplasticity, paying attention and concentrating better really can change your brain's ability and, by extension, how you go about things. Even allowing for all the variables – personality, temperament, intelligence, age, etc. – you can change your brain's function by the way you behave, and your behaviour by the way your brain functions. 'That's what learning is', says Professor Richard Davidson, director of the Laboratory of Affective Neuroscience at the University of

Wisconsin-Madison in the US. 'Anything that changes behaviour changes the brain.'

Given what we now know about the brain's ability to respond to our behaviour, learning to concentrate is a much more attractive idea and one that should perhaps be deliberately taught in schools, as important a life skill as reading or writing. The difference concentration makes can be clearly seen in the work of psychologist Richard Nisbett from the University of Michigan, who has looked closely at cultural attitudes of American students, and says: 'A Chinese-American with an IQ of 100 achieves at the level of a white American with an IQ of 120. This is a direct result of their more highly focused attitude when it comes to their schoolwork.'

Try differently

So often when what we have to do is routine, it can be boring, or consist of little to create the sort of interest and enthusiasm that keeps us engaged and motivated, which means we can easily slip into the habit of approaching anything with the same slightly half-hearted attitude. But it's important to remember that if you always do what you've always done, you will always get what you've always got. Same practice, same results. Don't try harder to make the changes you want: try differently.

Our internal voice and old habits are some of the biggest problems when it comes to learning to concentrate. Why, your brain says, should I concentrate on this when it is not interesting and I don't want to? I can't see the point. This is something that often affects schoolchildren or students, but can affect any of us who occasionally have to work on something we don't identify with or find remotely interesting. When this happens, or when we get a mental block about something, it's easy to miss the route through the mundane to the more interesting, to the stage when engagement makes concentration more possible.

Like a lot of children, I hated maths at school. In retrospect I don't think I was particularly well taught, but the upshot of my mindset was that I couldn't see the point of learning trigonometry because, as I once blithely told an infuriated teacher, I wasn't going to need it to go shopping. Not being able to do maths also made me feel stupid because I couldn't do it, which was a disincentive. But rather than master it – by concentrating and applying myself – I just dismissed it as irrelevant. What I couldn't see then was the pleasure of the intellectual tussle needed to create mathematical solutions that might be relevant to a more creative way of thinking in maths, and possibly in other areas. It had no attraction to me then, and no one at the time was able to convince me otherwise; it had no context, and I could find no frame of reference for it. It was only years later, when reading William Boyd's novel *The New Confessions*, which features a mathematical prodigy called Hamish Malahide, that I realized, for the first time, how engaging maths could be.

Creating interest

How, then, is it possible to create interest – thereby enabling concentration – in something you find boring? Some people seem to be able to just 'knuckle down' and get on with it. What they are doing is actually helping their ability to concentrate by focusing on just this one thing. Whether through innate or learned wisdom, they have found the secret: that is, you go on doing something until it starts tweaking your imagination and internal connections. The aim is to stimulate your internal mental activity, creating context and points of reference so that it relates to something you understand and becomes interesting, while creating interest in its own right.

The opposite and unsuccessful way of trying to do this is to rely on external stimulus to create interest. By this I mean doing a handful of things – instant messaging, listening to music, multitasking – that you think will help you do something you find boring by distracting you from your boredom while you do it. It won't make what you have to do any more interesting, but it will distract you from engaging with it until it is interesting enough to stimulate your internal life, enabling you to concentrate.

This is often the mistake teenagers make with homework. It doesn't interest them, they don't want to do it and they inhibit the possibilities of concentration by trying to do the work against a backdrop of distraction. Result: one poor piece of poorly remembered work that has been poorly executed. And it is unlikely that doing it in this half-hearted way has transferred any of the useful information from working memory into the long-term memory stores, making the whole process, effectively, a complete waste of time. You may have done your maths homework, but in such a way that the skill required to do it will be impossible to access at some future date. By not focusing, not only have you actually denied yourself from the possibility of concentrating but, and perhaps more importantly, not concentrating has denied you the possibility of retaining a useful learning experience.

Creating interest also allows for the possibility of enjoying the process of what you have to do. Once you start to enjoy something, it becomes easier to concentrate. However, if you don't put enough into the initial process, you won't stand a chance. It's a bit like swimming. It's not actually possible to swim unless you are immersed in water. You just can't swim in six inches of water: you would have restricted movement, and the possibility of floating, let alone swimming, does not exist. You need at least six times that much; then it's possible.

Say you are attending a seminar or lecture that will be useful to you. The topic may not be one that immediately 'grabs' you but, in order to pass an exam or gain a further qualification – one that will enable you to move towards something you do want to do – you know that you will benefit, in the long term, from forcing yourself to attend and spend all day sitting in a stuffy lecture room. So, do you sit there silently texting from your phone, or emailing on your BlackBerry, or daydreaming, or listening to music on your iPod? Not if you want to concentrate and benefit from the experience. You will have to find some way to make sure you can engage with what the speaker is saying, so that you concentrate and remember what you hear and see. If the speaker is dynamic, with lots of relevant anecdotes and a stimulating PowerPoint presentation, it will be easier to concentrate. But if that's not the case, you will have to work harder.

Help yourself to concentrate

Given this situation – the uninteresting subject matter, the low-key presentation, the stuffy environment – how can you help yourself to concentrate? No one says it's easy, but times when you are going to need to concentrate even when you would rather drift off into a pleasant daydream are likely to occur on numerous occasions during a lifetime. So it's worth knowing about some tools you can use.

○ First off, it's always worth doing some preparation beforehand if you can. Is there some background reading or an internet search that you could do on the subject? Is there someone else, a colleague or a friend, who knows a bit about this (maybe they've taken the seminar/done the course themselves), to whom you can talk in order to get a bit of background knowledge? Coming completely cold to something makes it more difficult to engage with it straight away.

○ Take notes. They don't need to be extensive, and you don't have to write down every word – there may be handouts that cover some of it – but keeping a note of specifics, something you'd like to follow up or something you don't quite understand, as well as any *aides memoires*, can be helpful in keeping you focused. Also, the physical process of writing, making a connection between thought and deed, helps you focus and retain information, supporting your concentration. Just be aware that with pen and paper in hand, there may be a temptation to doodle, which may then tempt your mind into wandering, rather than staying focused.

O When it comes to remembering key information, you can try creating mnemonics or acronyms, shorthand ways of making information more easily retrievable. The process of doing so will help you concentrate on the actual information.

O Often on occasions like this, there is a question-and-answer opportunity later on or at the end of the presentation. Make a note of any questions as they arise, not least because in questioning the information you will be engaging with it, which will automatically help your concentration. Also, making a note of questions as they arise will help you formulate them, and they will also provide a useful reference point when you review your notes later, indicating areas in which you may want to elicit more information on which to build in your own time.

Using these tools within this specific situation is one thing, but they are useful activities in their own right and can be applied elsewhere. Once you get into the habit of approaching situations in this organized way, you will find it becomes a useful discipline when you want to concentrate. This approach is transferable to other situations because it is a way of focusing. So, even if you don't actually take physical notes, your mind will be geared up to receiving information in an enquiring and engaged way, which will help support your concentration. You will be more organized in your thoughts, and less easily distracted.

Organization

How often do you start something without thinking it through? Or start something knowing that you're likely to be interrupted any minute, or knowing that you don't really have

◎ ORGANIZE YOURSELF

○ Make a list, so that you can actually see what it is you are trying to achieve. A list will also ensure you don't forget something crucial, and will relieve any anxiety that you may have about the possibility you will overlook something important.

○ From this initial list, decide on your priorities. This will stop you jumping from one thing to another, which can make you feel anxious. Once you know what your priorities are, and, just as crucially, which of those tasks are time sensitive, you are more likely to stay on top of your schedule.

○ Work through each task as far as you can before moving on to the next.

○ Create some sort of routine so that you don't get overwhelmed by the curse of the 24/7 mentality that says you never need stop. You need to balance yourself so that you can work effectively, without exhausting yourself. You need to factor in some downtime in order to be able to concentrate most effectively. Being overtired, as we have seen time and again, substantially reduces your ability to concentrate.

enough time to do justice to what you want to do? Or start something when you are really too tired to do it properly? No wonder you can't concentrate. A bit of organization and planning of your time can make all the difference to how you are able to really focus and concentrate. In much the same way as reducing physical clutter will help you, reducing the clutter in your head by taking a few simple steps to organize yourself will stop you rushing at things, help reduce the necessity to multitask and generally work to enhance better concentration to see you to the end of the task.

Do you have enough information to start?

Because we are, by nature, impatient/hard pressed/too busy – delete as appropriate – we often jump into a task without first thinking it through, organizing ourselves (see above) or garnering the information we need to concentrate on it. How often have you tried to do something in a hurry, messed it up, and had to start again? We all do it, and can waste a lot of time doing so. 'More haste, less speed' is the old adage and there is a good reason behind it.

Make a point of allowing yourself the space to prepare to concentrate, rather than thinking concentration will happen automatically when you start doing something. Ideally, when we want to get something done, we should make a point of focusing on just that one thing, but we have got into the habit of trying to accomplish several things at once, or in a hurry, and then we wonder why the ability to concentrate seems so elusive. Old habits die hard, but this is your chance to consciously re-visit how you do things, and find new and different ways that are more beneficial to you.

Motivation

What is your motivation for a particular task? Sometimes the answer is easy. Here are some examples: I like cooking because I like food and eating, and the social side of sharing a meal with friends. Going for a run is good because, after I have done it, I feel physically great. Playing that computer game online is fun because I am interacting with my friends, and it's increasingly rewarding as I get better at it. Playing Chopin's *Grande Valse Brillante* on the piano gives me a sense of accomplishment. I really enjoy playing chess because it challenges me.

The motivation for all these tasks is obvious, but what about the things you have never tried or done? You won't know what it is you could gain from doing them and, the first time you try something new, you probably won't gain much from it either. If you tried something and you immediately enjoyed it, you would be more likely to do it again. But there are occasions when the first effort is completely demoralizing because it's difficult, or hard, and the rewards – the same rewards that might motivate you in the future – are not obvious. Just about everyone (adult) that I've met who loves skiing, for example, tells me that they hated it at first. So what was it that kept them going long enough to get to the point where it was pleasurable and fun? Something motivated them, and it was the finding of that personal motivation, whatever it was (wanting to master the sport so they could ski with their partner, perhaps, or enjoying the ambience, or competitiveness), that motivated them enough to persevere.

Understanding what motivates you generally, and what might motivate you regarding a specific task on which you would like to improve your concentration, can be very helpful. Sometimes it's even useful to motivate yourself by creating tangible rewards. For example, allocate a period of time to concentrate 100 per cent, and then reward yourself with a break or a ten-minute phone call to a friend – anything that is a deferred pleasure can help to increase your motivation.

Purpose

Often we do things just because they need doing, and we do them without any particular sense of purpose. For example, the washing up is a routine, rather tedious task that just needs doing, usually at least once a day! However, there is an unacknowledged sense of purpose to doing it. Not doing it would mean that eventually we would have nothing to cook with or eat from, and dirty dishes left unattended will become unsanitary and a health hazard; so there are very good reasons for doing the washing up. There is a sense of purpose, however remote, and it is time sensitive – it's not something we can put off indefinitely.

Finding a sense of purpose will help motivate you, but there are, of course, often things about which we have a choice and, if concentration is difficult, we may choose not to do them. For example, we have three weeks to get a report written. It's not very interesting, so it will probably get left until the last minute when a sense of purpose will be artificially created by the now looming dreaded deadline and perhaps the fear of someone else's disapproval, rather than the pleasure of doing it. Some people always work in this way and will tell you it works for them. This is fine, as long as nothing else crops up! But often, and yet again, because the task has been left to the last minute, time pressure and anxiety about its impending deadline makes concentration difficult, and although the job does get done, it will have been rushed and not be as good a job as we know we are actually capable of. All round, this is not a great outcome.

Creating a sense of purpose can be done by approaching a task in a practical way, by taking the bigger picture – the conclusion or outcome of the task – and working backwards, identifying the steps in between. So, for example, if your task involves writing an essay or a report:

○ Establish what the topic is and what question your work needs to answer.
○ Brainstorm your subject – make a mind map (see page 89) – and then edit out and delete any information not immediately relevant to the subject, unless it illustrates a point in some way.
○ Decide what information you need to answer the question/s raised.
○ Who has this information? Do you need to read around

your subject/talk to people/research the details before
you start?

○ Ask yourself what is your purpose – to document, explain,
argue, persuade? This will influence your choice of
information that supports your work.

○ Decide how much time do you need to do the preparatory
work, before you begin writing.

○ Break down the structure into headings, which will start to
create the shape of your work and help you make sure you
do not miss any important information out.

○ Write the body of your text.

○ Even if you drafted your introduction earlier, always write
it last when you know what you are introducing.

○ Write your conclusion.

Suddenly the work you need to do has a tangible shape, and
you have accessed the 'how to' of actually doing of it. Along the
way, through this process, you have created small purposeful
tasks that will lead you on to the next stage and the next. Now
that you have a purpose, the process seems much less daunting
and, by concentrating on each stage at a time, you can accomplish the task with ease.

What's more, you've also learned that the tools required to
help you concentrate are not so difficult to find and use. Now
you just have to go on using them.

Conclusion

○ **Next time you tell yourself 'I'm having trouble concentrating' or 'I must
try harder', change the words of that critic in your head to 'Don't try
harder, try differently'.** Creating a genuine interest in something
you want or need to concentrate on is a really good way of
trying differently. If it's a subject you know nothing about
or hated at school, find someone who does know about

it and can share their enthusiasm with you. Enthusiasm is catching and trying differently is a really good way to start concentrating differently.

○ **Don't ever start a task which you need to give your full attention to, and concentrate on, knowing that you don't have what you need** (the reports, the statistics, the background information) to get to grips with the content and start concentrating.

○ **Avoid the temptation to multitask,** which means you might work your way through several tasks or activities but you'll do none of them well and your powers of concentration will slip as you try to focus on too many things at the same time.

○ **Know your purpose.** If you know where you're going with a project and what you want the outcome to be, you'll be much more likely to stay engaged and focused, and concentrating will be easier than if you start something with a voice in the back of your mind saying, 'Hey, where's this going? Do you know because I sure as hell don't.' Having or identifying a purpose is highly motivating, will help you see a task or activity through and will show up in all areas of your life, not least your ability to concentrate better and for longer.

CHAPTER NINE
Specific exercises to improve concentration

Men acquire a particular quality by constantly acting
in a particular way . . . you become just by performing
just actions, temperate by performing temperate actions,
brave by performing brave actions.

Aristotle

I f he had known how far our lifestyle with its constant distractions would have evolved by the twenty-first century, Aristotle might also have included 'and men learn concentration by concentrating'. Like just about anything else in life, from playing the violin to playing football, concentration can be improved through the doing of it. While an element of natural ability can create the first creative push towards excellence, nothing is achieved without extensive practice – remember the researchers who have estimated that 10,000 hours, or three hours a day for ten years, is the required input to reach true expertise in any field you care to think of. So, if you get into the habit of concentrating, creating opportunities to concentrate well, you will begin to find that you are concentrating on what you do more naturally.

Bad habits, good habits

With concentration, sometimes it's a question of simply replacing bad habits with good, but more often it's the repeated doing of something that will accomplish an improvement. Sometimes all you will need to start to improve your powers of concentration is to identify those bad habits that are getting in the way – a penchant for daydreaming, or procrastination, or checking emails every two minutes, for example. Once you've identified these you will be able to remove those blocks to better concentration and will find yourself more focused on doing what you now know will benefit your activity, rather than detract from it.

Some people will tell you that, for example, they chew their fingernails when they are concentrating. In fact, chewing their fingernails serves as a distraction and gets in the way of real concentration, because that process is stimulating another bit of your brain, forcing it into competition with your efforts to concentrate. What's actually happening, when people chew their fingernails, is that they find it reassuring to have what is, essentially, a form of oral comfort, because they find the effort of trying to concentrate quite stressful. Recognizing this means you can begin to unravel what might be getting in the way of your ability to concentrate. Maybe you haven't garnered enough information on which to focus, so anxiety about your lack of information is distracting you. Find out what you need to know, make notes, organize yourself and focus on it, bit by bit, so that you are helping your concentration rather than dissipating it.

If you are someone who despairs of ever being able to concentrate, then the exercises and suggestions outlined in this chapter should help – as long as you do them! You may be someone who has absorbed other people's ideas about them over the years. How many times were you told you were a 'butterfly brain', never able to focus or easily distracted? In reality you may have had quite good-enough concentration abilities, but constantly being given this message reinforced the idea that you were unable to concentrate, so you began to believe it. Whatever the truth of the situation, you can change it now by positively reinforcing another message that says: I can concentrate. I know how to concentrate. I can learn to concentrate. Doing specific exercises will help you reassure yourself that you can learn to concentrate.

Childhood games

Do you remember some of the games you played as a child that involved listening, remembering and repeating? If you played them at school, organized by your teacher, you can be sure that this was a deliberate attempt to help you focus and concentrate, work better in class and – your teacher hoped – learn your lessons more easily. Did you ever play Chinese whispers, and laugh as the message got completely distorted along the way? Did you play the memory game, when you had to memorize a selection of items on a tray and write them down when the tray was covered up? Then the tray returned with a number of items removed, and you had to identify which ones were missing? Or the alphabet game, where everyone added an item beginning with the next letter in the alphabet to a shopping list, and you had to remember and recite that growing list in the correct order? As you will see, some of those memory games are actually all about concentration. You may have found these 'games' easy or hard back then; you may remember classmates who were very good at it, or not; you may also have forgotten the good habits you got into then, but there's no reason why you can't revisit some of those games and get your concentration skills in better shape again.

Learning to concentrate is really a question of persistently engaging and re-engaging your attention. Creative, imaginative thinking is, by its very nature, digressive, but this same facility for digression can get in the way of concentration. So, by learning how to resist digression at will, and by practising deliberately returning your attention to a focal point, you will, eventually, be able to concentrate at will.

It doesn't matter what age you are or why you choose to do these exercises; everyone can benefit. The brain has a far greater neuroplasticity than scientists previously gave it credit for. Research over the last ten years has shown that the brain's ability to adapt and change throughout life is one of its greatest assets and one we can exploit. I once interviewed a professor of mathematics who had agreed to take part in some functional MRI studies at his university. Prior to having his brain watched on the MRI scanner, while solving mathematical problems, he signed his consent and was asked, 'If by chance we find any sort of anomaly, do you want to know?' 'Yes', he said. Greatly to his – and the researcher's – surprise, the MRI showed explicit evidence that at some point over the last few years, he had suffered a major stroke. He had had no symptoms to suggest this had been the case, although the damage to his brain was plain to see on the MRI scan. But here was a man who used his brain in a highly specialized way, studying and teaching degree-level mathematics – he was also an accomplished musician and played regularly in an orchestra – whose brain's function had been completely (as far as he could tell) unaffected by the area of damage caused by the stroke. So we know that neurons respond positively to stimulus and can compensate for damage and deficiencies elsewhere in the brain. While a lot of the brain is highly specialized, there is still enormous scope for neuroplasticity and, it turns out, powers of compensation for those parts that have been damaged, destroyed or lost.

Neurogenesis

One of the other great discoveries of the late twentieth century was that the brain was also capable of generating new brain cells. Previously, it was thought that we were born with every last brain cell we would ever have, and that no more could be created. This turns out not to be the case. Neurogenesis, to give it its medical name, is the creation of new brain cells from precursor cells that occur in the hippocampus, which is so important for memory. Although there had been some evidence of this from work done on the brains of birds and other animals, it was eventually identified in human brains from the tenacious work of a Swedish stem cell neuroscientist, Peter Eriksson, from the Sahlgrenska University Hospital, Gothenburg. The biochemical marker that had been used in animal experiments couldn't, ethically, be used for human experimentation for this purpose at the time. However, elsewhere approved medical studies were being carried out in terminal cancer patients – where new cells are created by the cancer – and this same biochemical marker was being used to try to evaluate the effectiveness of treatment, because it would flag up neurogenesis. Eriksson's scientific assumption was that if the brain were capable of neurogenesis, these new cells would show evidence of the same biochemical marker that was being used to identify new cancer cells. So he asked if he could have the brains of these patients, after their death, to examine and see if there was – as he thought there might be – any evidence of neurogenesis.

This work was also being explored in the US by the eminent neuroscientist Professor Fred Gage, at the Salk Institute for Biological Studies, California. After extensive study, and ruling out the possibility that new cells in the brain could be secondary cancer cells, the scientists finally got their 'Eureka!' moment in 1998. The brain was capable of neurogenesis. Gage said:

> All the brains had evidence of new cells exactly in the area where we had found neurogenesis in other species. And we could prove through chemical analysis that they were mature neurons. The neurons were born in the patients when they were in their fifties and seventies, and these neurons stayed alive until the people died. That was the first evidence for neurogenesis in the adult human brain. So now we know that in some areas of the brain, new neurons are being made all the time. It was a surprise because

we thought the brain was stagnant. But in this region of the hippocampus, there are these little baby cells that are dividing, and over time, they mature and migrate into the circuitry and become a full-blown adult neuron with new connections. And this is occurring throughout life. The finding brought us an important step closer to the possibility that we have more control over our own brain capacity than we ever thought possible.

What was also becoming clear from continuing research with mice was that voluntary exercise was as crucial to neurogenesis as environmental enrichment. So not only did the old adage 'use it or lose it' apply to neurogenesis, but physical activity is crucial too. Gage says:

We think that voluntary exercise increases the number of neural cells that divide and give rise to new neurons in the hippocampus. But we think it is environmental enrichment that supports the survival of these cells. Usually, 50 per cent of the new cells reaching the dentate gyrus of the hippocampus die. But if the animal lives in an enriched environment, many fewer of the cells die. Environmental enrichment doesn't seem to affect cell proliferation and the generation of new neurons, but it can affect the rate and the number of cells that survive and integrate into the circuitry.

Much of this work has been continued through the close collaboration between Western neuroscientists and the Buddhist monks of Tibet, through the Mind and Life Institute, founded by the Chilean cognitive neuroscientist Francisco Varela, businessman Adam Engle and the Dalai Llama in 1987. What is becoming increasingly clear from this work is that how we use our minds can actually change the function and performance of our brains.

Exercises

The following exercises are ways of identifying and extending your concentration skills. Start by doing them when you feel well rested and alert, somewhere peaceful and quiet, until they become familiar and easy. Then challenge yourself further by doing them with the distraction of the radio on, or when you are feeling tired or stressed. Once you have become well versed in these exercises, you should be able to focus on them even in difficult circumstances. In fact, being able to focus and concentrate on them may actually help to relieve stress by disengaging your mind for a while, as if in some sort of active meditation.

SITTING STILL

This exercise is more difficult than it sounds – not least because we very rarely do nothing at all. It requires considerable physical and mental discipline – and concentration. If you find it difficult at first, and it is quite likely that you will, persevere, because it will pay dividends in helping you to stay calm and focus, and will become one of an arsenal of skills you can utilize *in extremis*, or develop into a capacity for meditation.

Start by sitting in a relaxed position, upright in a chair, without slumping. Don't cross your legs; instead sit with your feet flat on the floor, your hands resting palm upwards on your thighs. Use your core muscles to support you, relax your shoulders (you may need to scrunch them upwards first, then drop them down and do this several times to ensure they are relaxed), lengthen through the back of the neck and drop your chin a little. Try to breathe using your diaphragm and stomach muscles, not from the upper chest. Now sit still. Be aware of areas of discomfort but, having previously adjusted your position, don't move again; just register the thought and move on. Be aware of any involuntary muscular movements, but consciously relax the limb in which they occur, and move on. Stay concentrated on your body, rather than drifting away with your thoughts, and do this for five minutes. Don't extend the time until you are really comfortable with five minutes.

Once you start to practise sitting still regularly, you should find it gets easier the more you do it. Once you can manage fifteen minutes, use this as your optimum practice time; there is no need to extend it further.

BLACK SPOT

The simplest exercise, which can be done virtually anywhere, is to fix your gaze on a small object. This works best where there are no associations connected to it, so sticking a black spot – about two inches in diameter – on a plain wall is perfect. Consciously leave to one side any thoughts that arise, returning again and again to the focus of your attention. This is also the basis of any meditative practice. You need to do this for only three minutes a day to start flexing your ability to concentrate.

Over time, you can develop this practice by drawing a square around the dot in your imagination. Then you can concentrate on the space between the lines of the square and the dot, all the time consciously drawing your attention away from any digressive thoughts and back to the dot and square and the space between.

CLOCK EXERCISE

For this you will need an old-fashioned clock, not digital, with hands and a second hand. Start with the second hand at the twelve and then concentrate on watching it travel around the clock face, without letting any distracting thoughts intervene. Every time this happens, stop and wait until the second hand is back at the twelve, and start again. Initially, if you can concentrate for three seconds, you will be doing well. It's much more difficult than it sounds, and it will make you really appreciate the discipline it takes to learn how to concentrate, and what a difference it could make to how you approach life and work once you can.

Slowly build up your ability to suspend all thought and concentrate on the clock hand, and once you reach thirty seconds, try again – but with your eyes shut. Open them immediately a digressive thought arises, and see how far you've got on the clock. This time, it might be your internal voice that distracts you, or a greater awareness of the noise around you once your eyes are shut. In any event, over time, you will find that you can improve your ability to do this with relative ease.

COUNTING

Start with the number 1,000 and count backwards in your head in sevens: that is, 1,000, 993, 986, 979, 972, 965 and so on. You will probably find that at first it is really quite difficult, and you will feel irritated and disgruntled by being unable to do it with any proficiency. If you are a visual learner, you may find that you 'see' the numbers in your head; if you are a tactile learner, you may find yourself using your fingers; and if you are an auditory learner you may find it easier to say the numbers out loud.

Once you have got really good at this, challenge yourself by doing it with the radio on. Then, change the challenge by altering the number you subtract – from seven to five or eleven, for example. Otherwise, you will begin to know the numbers by rote, rather than actively subtracting them.

SPELLING

Without writing the letters down, take a word and spell it backwards. Start with quite short words and build up to longer ones. If you take a word you are familiar with, like 'box', 'cup' or 'dog', your brain will soon get the idea. Move on to longer words like 'shoe', 'month', 'black' and 'phone'; then words like 'driving', 'postal', 'message', 'caffeine' and 'effort'; then words like 'benefit', 'sausages', 'parallel', 'radiator' and 'vehicle'; then words like 'business', 'mechanism', 'excessive' and 'concentration'! Once you get into the habit of concentrating on this, it

JIGSAW PUZZLES

Doing jigsaws puzzles is excellent for developing concentration skills. Start with a relatively small number of pieces, before moving on to the 5,000-piece version of John Constable's painting of *The Hay Wain* – it's probably easier not to start with something as complicated as this, especially if it has been a long while since you did a jigsaw. You need to do this for a sustained period of time. Five minutes here and there between other tasks, or while you are watching the TV or listening to the radio, won't be as helpful to you as focusing on it exclusively for an extended period of time.

will become easier, but you need to build on small, short words to begin with and create more of a challenge for yourself using longer words as you get better at it. You may even improve your ability to spell!

COUNTING WORDS

Without touching the page, count up how many words there are on a page of text. Develop this by moving on to counting how many times the word 'the' appears on a page. As you improve with this, on a new page count up how many times the words 'the' and 'and' appear – so that you end up with two different sums at the end of the page. Again, you will be developing your ability to concentrate and then challenging and building on it.

CROSSWORDS

Some people seem to be amazingly good at crosswords, while others loathe them. What you tend to find is that those who like crosswords are rather good at them and also that they have been doing them for years. There's a clue there. They like them because they can do them. Even when they are challenging –

and they enjoy that too! And a big part of their ability to do them comes from having done them regularly for a long while. You often hear of elderly people who are still doing *The Times* crossword in their eighties. When you've been doing something regularly for sixty years, being able to concentrate on it is not so hard. Many daily newspapers do a crossword, and often they do an 'easy' crossword and a 'cryptic'. If you are a newcomer to crosswords, start with the easy ones and go on to cryptic ones as you progress. Crossword aficionados often have their favourite crossword compilers, and will recognize the style of the clues, which adds to their feeling of engagement and inclusion. In addition there is the feel-good, reward factor of completing a crossword, which raises endorphins in the brain – all of which are factors in helping concentration.

SUDOKU AND OTHER PUZZLES
Like crosswords, doing Sudoku and similar puzzles, which both exercise but focus the brain and demand concentration, will be helpful. However, the trick here is that you have to stick at the puzzle when it becomes challenging. Don't make a half-hearted stab at it and then give up when the going gets tough. Very often people will flit from puzzle to puzzle, which may be fun and relatively engaging, but won't necessarily help improve your concentration. If you do puzzle games in this way, you are probably using them as a short-term distraction from another task, rather than as an opportunity to engage your brain's ability to concentrate.

GAMES WITH OTHERS
Remember how you played 'I went on holiday and in my bag I packed . . .' and, using the letters of the alphabet, you worked through it with by naming something with that letter? Each person has to add something, and everyone has to remember what went before. So, 'I went on holiday and in my bag I packed an apple, a bathing suit, a crochet set, some dollars, an

encyclopaedia, a fishing rod', and so on. This exercise is also good for improving memory skills.

You can use a variety of similar themes; 'My grandmother went shopping and she bought . . .' is another. You can make your own rules, choosing a particular theme, such as food or clothes, or opting for something more outrageous and unlikely, such as wild animals. With a group of people, it's always interesting to see how differently they will approach the game, and what skills they draw upon to do it successfully. Interestingly, younger people often struggle at this game, perhaps from never having played it before or because they have never, like the older generation, had to learn things by rote. There are also always distractions in this game caused by the participants themselves, as people disagree on items, or say something funny that makes everyone laugh – so being able to concentrate can be difficult!

I-SPY

Unless you have young children and participate in long car journeys, you are unlikely to have played I-Spy for a while – and while this is not necessarily a recommendation to start now, I-Spy is a good example of a simple game that focuses the mind and forces you to concentrate for a while. This is, of course, a good game for your children or grandchildren – and perfect for long car journeys. It is a sociable group activity, it demands some intellectual application and with younger children it teaches the alphabet and observation as well as concentration skills (along with taking turns, participation, rules of the game, etc.).

VISUALIZATION EXERCISES

We are very good at grabbing information visually. We are used to seeing things peripherally, out of the corner of our eye, and often we think this is the whole picture. We seldom, consciously, take a really good look at things. Have you ever witnessed an event and then compared what you saw with friends who were there at the same time? Surprisingly enough, there may be as many different views and opinions about the event as the number of friends that were present to witness it with you. We tend to see things in different ways partly because we have different points of interest.

Without being too sexist, a man is more likely to tell you the make of a car that just flashed past than a woman; whereas a woman may be better able to remember details of the dress her sister wore to a family wedding. If you are interested in people, you are more likely to remember their eye colour. But generally speaking, unless they have a direct relevance to us, we tend not to concentrate on details. Have you ever inadvertently witnessed an accident or a crime, and realized that if you had to give a witness statement or a description of events, you would find it hard to provide actual details? Some people are, by nature or inclination, more observant than others, but generally we are notoriously bad at seeing things, because we seldom concentrate on the information we receive visually unless it is of relevance to us personally. This is a lost opportunity when it comes to flexing your concentration 'muscle'. For by deliberately enhancing your visualization skills, you will help to improve your concentration.

You can also do this by looking at a picture of something unfamiliar to you. It's important that this isn't a picture of a place or person you know, because if it is you will have memories and opinions and all sorts of information about it already accessible to you that will be a distraction and will make your attention waver and digress. Focus on it closely, concentrating on the detail, for a minute. Then, without looking at it, spend the next few minutes trying to recall as much as you can about the picture you have just been scrutinizing. You may want to make a note of what you can recall about the image, and then check back against the picture itself to see how accurately you remembered it. You may find you start to use techniques to remember information, making a mental note of colours or objects, for instance, to help you recall them accurately later. This is all part of concentrating, to the exclusion of anything else, and will enable you to function well at this task.

Another form of visualization is purely imaginative – you can do this with your eyes shut! But it must have a form and structure; otherwise it would be more accurate to call this exercise 'daydreaming'. Sometimes it forms the basis of a 'guided meditation' and you can buy commercial audiotapes that provide an experience of this. However, for the purpose of exercising your ability to concentrate, you need to do this yourself and be quite disciplined. Here is a format you can use.

VISUALIZATION TECHNIQUE

Lie on your back in a comfortable position, possibly with a pillow under your knees for comfort, and consciously relax your body. Breathe gently in and out a few times, from your stomach and diaphragm muscles rather than your upper chest, to calm yourself. Then start your visualization, the purpose of which is to concentrate on the journey you are about to make in your head. Imagine a walk with which you are familiar. This can be a rural or urban setting, and you can be walking for pleasure or for a purpose (possibly a walk you do on your way to work, or to a friend's house). Even though the walk is familiar to you, try not to engage in any emotions about it because the focus for this purpose is to concentrate on your surroundings. First the time of day: morning, afternoon, early evening (it should be light enough for your surroundings to be visible). What time of year is it? Is it spring, with lots of new, green growth, or autumn, with its dying golden leaves? It doesn't matter which it is; what you are doing is simply providing a backdrop to your visualization. The weather: is it warm, sunny, cold, raining, windy?

▶

What are you wearing as a consequence? Can you feel the sensation of the sun on your face, the wind in your hair? Are you walking on tarmac or grass? Are you struggling up a hill or walking along a straight path? Is the path open, or are there trees and other plants? What can you hear – birdsong, distant traffic, people's voices, the sound of water?

Once you've got your background visualized, take the walk. Visualize what you see along the way, imagining the surroundings in as much detail as you can. However familiar the route, you have probably walked it many times with your mind on other things; now really visualize the detail. Take your time and notice the colours of what you see, the rich variety, even the way the light falls and the shadows if any. Visualize it as if you are noticing for the first time what you are seeing. Really look at it as you visualize this walk.

Doing this for the first time, you may feel as if you are rushing through it, trying to accomplish a task, rather than visualizing the process. Don't worry: this is because you are trying to counteract a pattern of behaviour that, in the past, has probably stood in the way of your concentration. We can sometimes get so hung up on what we are trying to achieve that the achievement becomes the goal, while the process of achieving it gets marginalized. What we are aiming for is a process of achieving, through concentration, something that will help improve the outcome – we will be more effective through this process rather than less so. However, when we first start to unlearn old ways of doing things, and learn new ones, it can feel clunky and odd. Remember when you first started learning to drive a car, and how alien that felt? Or learned to knit? Or played the piano? It's sometimes as well to remind ourselves that it takes time to become proficient at something. Stay with it and practise until it becomes not only familiar but a more comfortable and, in the end, more successful way of doing it.

FOCUSING

Sometimes you will have to make a real effort to concentrate. For example, you may be at a lecture where the presentation is poor but you know the content will be of value to you. How are you going to maintain concentration when it's all too easy for your thoughts to wander? In this case, focus on the lecturer. Avoid looking around you or noticing your other colleagues or the ambience of the room you are in. Actively avoid distraction. Keep your focus on the lecturer, and think about what he or she is saying. If you take notes, paraphrase them rather than writing out statements verbatim. Make a note of any questions you might want to ask later, to focus your attention on the subject matter. If you have been given any handouts, don't read them now, which will distract you, but review them later. In your head, consider the lecturer down a tunnel through which you are looking. Make connections in your head with what you know and what you are hearing; you are doing this to help reinforce your concentration so that you are actively listening (and absorbing) what you are hearing. Don't start wondering about the lecturer's accent, dress sense or background. Consciously resist daydreaming by constantly ignoring your wandering thoughts; let them go without engaging with them.

Memory

Memory is closely linked to concentration so, generally speaking, seeking to improve one will improve the other, not least because of the stimulation this sort of activity provides for the hippocampus of the brain – so important for memory – and the support it provides for both neuroplasticity and neurogenesis.

Your memory doesn't involve just one part of your brain: it relies on a complex interplay between various areas of the brain. This is why – as we saw earlier – a certain smell, for example, can be very evocative and transport you back to a time when you first registered it, with all its associations, good or bad. The olfactory bulb, where smell is registered in the brain, is closely linked to the hippocampus – where new experiences are converted to neural pathways and stored for future access – and also the amygdala, which generates an emotional response. Smell can kick off very strong memories because of this close physical association in the brain. For years after I suffered bad morning sickness with my first pregnancy, I felt sick whenever I smelt basil, because I had used this herb in cooking while feeling very sick and emotional. This explains why some people like some smells that others find unpleasant or even repugnant. Because it is as children that we first experience many different smells, many childhood memories can be evoked by them. The smell of a bonfire might transport you back to the excitement, or fear, of a fireworks night party, depending on your experience of it. The smell of lavender may make you remember a favourite granny, and evoke feelings of warmth and security.

Long-term, short-term and working memory

The workings of the memory can be described as having two main components: short-term or working memory, and long-term memory. Short-term memory is what we use to remember a phone number, for example, which we have looked up in a directory and need to dial. We only need to remember it while we transfer our attention from the written information to our phone keypad. We can store information in this way for around forty-five seconds, and then the brain discards it. So, if you get interrupted or distracted while you are trying to do this, you won't retain the information accurately and will have to look that information up again. However, when you use a phone number often, the process of repeatedly dialling it means that, eventually, it will transfer into your long-term memory stores and you will never need to look it up again.

When testing short-term memory, scientists have found that we remember information with which we have an association better than that which is more abstract. For example, the numbers 10111986 may be tricky to remember, but if your birth date is 10 November 1986, then it will be easy to recall this particular sequence of numbers. Similarly, with a series of words, we can usually remember those with which we have an association better than those that are more abstract. So, in remembering a string of words, we are much more likely to remember those with which we have some sort of association. This explains why nouns like 'elephant', 'raspberry' or 'canary' are easier to remember than words like 'principal', 'sequence', or 'gradual': the former conjure up a visual image while the abstract nature of the latter means they do not.

We can also use strategies to help improve our short-term memory facility, making it easier to remember information. Two ways to do this are through repetition or 'rehearsal', when a name or number is repeated (either out loud or silently inside our heads) over and over again until it 'sticks' or, with numbers in particular, by 'chunking', where we break things down into chunks of information. So a random set of numbers become less random – for instance 8374601 becomes 837 4601. Indeed, many phone numbers are chunked into this configuration for easier use. We can also use tricks, or strategies, to help artificially create associations that will give information additional meaning, thus helping us to retain it. Names are a case in point. If you habitually meet a lot of people, or are bad at remembering names, it's useful to make a point of physical contact – shaking hands is the usual ploy – looking closely at the person to whom you are being introduced while being told their name. Make an internal note of something unique to that person to help you make a memorable association, and then repeat their name back and make sure you use it in conversation with them.

For information that needs to be retained over a length of time, short-term memory is no good. We need to be able to store and retrieve information, and for that to happen it needs to be 'encoded'. By associating new information with information already available, it gains meaning and relevance and can be stored for later retrieval. But this process can be vulnerable in its early stages.

When it comes to memory, concentration is a prerequisite. It's much more difficult to commit something to memory if you've not concentrated on it in the first place. True, some fleeting impressions will form part of your memories, but that's probably because they are related to a past memory, so they resonate with that, or because the fleeting impression you are not wholly concentrated on is part of a bigger picture with which you are already engaged and concentrated on. For example, you may be participating in an activity on which you are wholly concentrated, perhaps a competitive event like a football game, and while you won't remember instantly what the weather was like, you may be able to recall it while remembering the game itself.

Forgetting

So our memory can let us down, but forgetting things is a part of everyday life, especially if we are busy or distracted, or overloaded. 'Most forgetting occurs within an hour or so of learning or experiencing the thing being forgotten', says Dr Barry Gibb, PhD, a scientist and honorary fellow of University College London, who has studied communication between cells in the brain. He says:

> This may happen because we didn't really pay much atten-
> tion in the first place, or because no associations can be
> made with existing memories. If someone is introduced to

lots of people at a party, for instance, their names are likely to be quickly forgotten. Even if a name gets consciously processed, it's unlikely to stick unless it's repeated or can be pinned to some other memory – for example, the brother of a colleague shares a name with a friend and so on.

We have seen that the brain has a great plasticity and potential to improve. Functional MRI scanning has been one of the greatest gifts to our understanding of how much we can exploit its potential to work better for us now that it's actually possible to see which areas of the brain light up when stimulated in certain ways, and why. When it comes to memory, there are lots of things we can do to improve its capacity, but one of the most important is by concentrating better. Taking time to focus clearly on something, and blocking out other distractions, while the brain does its job, can clearly help. This is part of what lies behind techniques and strategies designed to improve memory – they force you to engage with and give meaning to what you are trying to remember.

Techniques to improve memory

It is possible to learn techniques to help your memory function better, and most of these tricks or strategies are about creating a context for something you want to remember. What they have in common is that they all require you to concentrate!

For example, if you want to remember a shopping list without writing it down, one memory technique recommends that you create a memorable context for each item. So if your shopping list is milk, carrots, bacon, self-raising flour, baked beans and coriander, then you simply link these items together in a story: along a river of milk float carrot boats with sails made of bacon, alongside a bank of growing (self-raising) flowers, where baked beans are picnicking under trees of coriander. Creating the story helps you to place the objects on your list into a meaningful, rather than a random, context, making them easier to remember.

Another recommended memory technique is based on your own home. Pick ten places or objects that live permanently in your home or office. Try and memorize these in some logical order. This may take you a while to accomplish, but it's your template from which you will work. When you want to remember a list of things, associate each item on the list with one of your ten places or objects. Use a combination of ways to do this, using mental imagery and even sounds, even in a nonsensical way. When you need to remember your list, simply walk around your home in your mind, and you will 'see' the items where you left them. Make the images as vivid as you can and you will discover that, with practice, this technique rarely fails. It was originally devised over 2,000 years ago by Roman orators, who would 'place' sections of their speech along a garden path, and then mentally walk through the garden remembering each topic in order as they gave the speech.

So your list around your house might be: the table by the front door; the mat on the hall floor; the third step of the stairs; the sink, fridge and oven in the kitchen; the light by your bed; the soap dish in the bathroom; the TV and CD player in the sitting room. Then to remember your shopping list, you would place the milk on the table by the front door; the carrots on the mat on the hall; the bacon on the third step of the stairs; self-raising flour in the sink; baked beans in the fridge; and coriander in the oven.

Conclusion

○ **The simplest way to start improving your concentration skills, having identified all the bad habits and distractions that make it so hard to concentrate, is to replace those habits with better ones.** Don't expect to do this overnight – it takes time, commitment and patience – but the rewards, including being able to concentrate at will, will be more than worth the effort.

○ **Remember those memory games you played as a child?** The long lists of items that worked their way through the letters of the alphabet or the trays crowded with different items that you had five minutes to memorize before the tray was covered again? Or even playing picture lotto with a child? These exercises are a simple and fun way to start to exercise your brain power, and by focusing on specifics, you'll soon find you get better with each go and can concentrate enough to retrieve that information and really enjoy the game.

○ **If you've ever tried just sitting still, then you'll already know it's not quite as easy as it sounds.** Your body will want to fidget. Your mind will fill itself with yesterday's (unfinished) 'to do' list and before you know it you'll be wriggling in your chair and reaching for a pen to write another 'to do' list. Sit through these distractions, push them out of your mind and try sitting still for long enough to start to feel what it is like to really focus and concentrate. Not only will you be surprised how quickly you can, once you overcome your initial resistance, develop this skill, but you'll reap the rewards, over and over, when you start to free yourself from the tyranny of what the ancient Yogis called 'the chattering monkeys' of the mind. And your powers of concentration will soon be second to none.

CHAPTER TEN
What else can you do?

Good conduct is the way in which life becomes
more meaningful, more constructive and more peaceful.
For this, much depends on our own behaviour and
our mental attitude.

The Dalai Lama

In solitude we give passionate attention to our lives,
to our memories, to the details around us.

Virginia Woolf

T he choices you start to make that will support your overall
aim of learning to concentrate better need to be integrated into your daily life, if they are to have a continuing
impact. We've seen how, when it comes to supporting your
brain's capacity to concentrate better, one thing that plays an
important part is regular physical exercise. It can actively help
neurogenesis, the brain's ability to generate new neurons, but
it also helps to engage the body and mind together in a way
that is enjoyable and challenging, keeping the mind and body
connected, and the mind focused and engaged. Whether your
choose to walk to work, play football twice a week, practise t'ai
chi every day or do a regular Pilates class, you can be reassured
that focusing your mind on exercising your body will help you

to concentrate better in other areas of your life. There are also other activities, like meditation, which create a pleasurable discipline that not only relaxes the mind but also enables us to extend and enhance the ability to concentrate. And it's when we avail ourselves of these opportunities, outside the tasks on which we want to concentrate better, that we will reinforce our efforts to improve concentration.

Breathing

A useful asset for many of the activities that we now know will enable us to focus body and mind is an understanding of how breathing can help, and, more specifically, how breathing can help connect the two. Paying attention to the breath is relevant to many activities from meditation to swimming to yoga, and with good reason. Because breathing is something we do automatically but can control at will (up to a certain point, because while we can pause and slow our breathing, we can never stop it) and because the way we breathe has an impact on other body systems, we can use it help calm our internal physical, and by extension, mental activity.

When we are stressed, anxious, frightened or angry, our breathing pattern speeds up and becomes quite shallow, and we breathe from the upper chest without fully inflating the lungs. This sort of breathing is quite useful in the short term, when you are running away from the proverbial sabre-toothed tiger for example, but it's a labour-intensive and tiring way to breathe all the time. However, many of us have, over the years, fallen into the habit of breathing this way all the time. We may sit for long hours in front of a computer with our shoulders tense and our rib cage tight, our breathing shallow. We may slouch in front of the television, or sit in conversation with a friend with our arms firmly crossed. This may not seem very important but because this is how we breathe when we are anxious, frightened or angry, if we breathe like this all the time, the body gets the wrong message and we can feel unnecessarily tense (and anxious, frightened or angry).

Our posture and breathing are also closely related. Poor posture will create poor breathing patterns – if you sit hunched, reducing your lung capacity, for example. Poor posture can impact on the gut and affect digestion, too. So by learning to breathe more effectively and in a way that conveys to the body that all is well, we can evoke more positive feelings in ourselves, while also providing more oxygen to our muscles and brain.

You can also use breathing exercises (such as the one described opposite) to centre your thoughts by concentrating on regulating the breath and relaxing your body. This is something you can easily achieve through practice on your own, and is not only a useful technique, in itself, but can be used to form the basis of future meditation practice. Once you begin to slow and steady your breathing, you stimulate your parasympathetic nervous system (PNS). Along with your sympathetic nervous system (SNS), the PNS is an arm of your autonomic nervous system that is outside your conscious control. Both your PNS and your SNS regulate your physical response to your emotional reactions. Your SNS behaves a bit like the accelerator on a car: once pressed, it releases the 'fight or flight' hormones, adrenalin and noradrenalin, to speed up the heart rate and prepare for action. The PNS, however, acts as a brake, triggering the release of a different neurotransmitter, acetylcholine, which slows and steadies the heart rate. The job of the autonomic nervous system is to keep these two, the SNS and the PNS, in balance, so that we can react when appropriate – perhaps to danger when the 'fight or flight' response is activated, but also to relax and recover after danger has passed. Keeping the body in balance can be influenced by how we feel, think and respond to life's challenges, and how we breathe will influence the body's response, too – which is why learning to breathe in this conscious way can be so useful to us when it comes to focusing our attention away from distractions.

⊕ BREATHING EXERCISE

○ Lie on your back, with your knees bent and arms at your sides, with either a book or a small cushion under your head to support your neck a little, making sure that your neck is long and the chin tucked in rather than jutting out (this is what Alexander Technique teachers call the constructive rest position).

○ Consciously relax your shoulders, and any other muscles that feel tense. Make sure you feel warm enough, relaxed and comfortable.

○ Gently rest one hand on your upper chest, and one on your abdomen. This will help you notice and regulate your pattern of breathing

○ Close your eyes. Breathing in through your nose, inhale gently and without force so that you feel not just the chest but your abdomen rising a little too. Pause. Then exhale gently through your mouth.

○ At first this breathing pattern will probably feel a little odd, strained even, but just stay with it until you find your own rhythm.

○ As you are naturally breathing a little deeper, you will take in more oxygen and this will automatically help slow your breathing. This fall in your breathing rate happens because it is actually the levels of carbon dioxide in your blood that are the trigger for breathing rates: the higher the level of carbon dioxide in the blood, the faster you breathe to try to get more oxygen into the system. (However, when over-breathing or hyperventilating occurs, as during a panic attack, over-oxygenation of the blood inhibits the breathing mechanism, which will make the body want to stop or slow breathing rates right down. This is what creates

▷

the breathing difficulties during a panic attack that are alleviated by breathing in and out of a paper bag, which increases the carbon dioxide levels in the blood to a more normal range.)

○ Continue breathing in this slow and steady way, keeping your awareness on the inhalation through the nose, and exhalation through the mouth. You will find that as you relax, your breath will slow to around twelve times a minute.

○ Sometimes it's helpful to silently intone the word 'in' on the in breath, and 'out' on the out breath. It sounds obvious, but it can help when you are trying to keep your mind focused on your breathing.

○ If you still find it difficult to focus solely on your breathing, with each breath you take visualize a pebble dropping into a pool of water and sinking through its depths.

○ Practise these breathing exercises once or twice daily, until you are so familiar with this new way of breathing that you can utilise it at will throughout the course of your day.

Heart coherence

Being aware of the different functions of the sympathetic and parasympathetic nervous systems, and how finding a balance within the body can help us manage our internal well-being, can be taken a step further with an understanding of heart coherence. The heart is much more than just a pump, whose electrical activity can be measured by an electrocardiogram or ECG. It also secretes small amounts of hormones: adrenalin if necessary, atrial natriuretic factor (ANF), which regulates blood pressure, and oxytocin (sometimes called the 'love hormone' because it is secreted by the body at orgasm, during breast-feeding and at other times of positive emotional response). The heart is a highly responsive piece of muscle, with a direct link to and from the brain, and it is possible not only to measure the electrical components of the heartbeat on an ECG, but also to measure heart rate variability (HRV), which shows up the variation in cardiac rhythm. There are two characteristic modes of cardiac rhythm: chaotic in response to the activity of the SNS and coherent in response to the activity of the PNS. When we are stressed, anxious or depressed, the SNS is persistently activated, increasing heart rate variability in its chaotic mode.

HRV was first described in 1992 by physicist Dan Winter, and study and development by the Institute of HeartMath in Colorado in the US has led to the creation of computer software that can detect it and show it on a monitor. The beauty of this is that you can learn to activate your PNS and thus influence your HRV so that it moves from a state of chaos to one of coherence. What's more, you can learn to do this at will, just by focusing first on your breathing, and then perhaps by concentrating on a maths problem – like the one where you deduct the number seven backwards from the number 1,000 and continue to deduct seven from the answer – or even by visualizing and revisiting in your mind a secure, happy memory. You can actually see your HRV moving to a state of coherence on the monitor, while experiencing what it is you are doing to achieve this, and with this biofeedback you can practise and improve on your skill. Not only is it good for your heart and your body's health, but it also provides you with proof of the effectiveness of creating this state of inner calm, which in turn frees up energy you can use to concentrate further. It is also this state of heart coherence that is experienced at moments of peak concentration, described as 'flow' (see page 133).

All of which goes some way to explain why major corporations such as Shell, BP, Hewlett Packard, Unilever and HSBC in the UK have instigated training courses in heart coherence for

> ### ◈ BENEFITS OF NATURE
>
> Increasing your exposure to the natural world – through a short walk every day, in a park if you live in a city – or even to the plants you have in your office can help reduce stress, improve concentration and enhance creativity. Green, the colour of nature, is soothing and the more natural, the better. Psychologically the colour green is also associated with the word 'go', so anything green has a positive effect.

their employees. Studies have shown that the health-promoting benefits of heart coherence include lowering blood pressure, lowering the damaging stress hormone cortisol (associated with poor concentration, memory loss and skin ageing) and raising levels of the 'youth hormone' DHEA (dehydropiandrosterone).

The Institute of HeartMath has also developed a small, hand-held device for personal use, called the emWave™ Personal Stress Reliever, which can be used to monitor and develop heart coherence, enabling the user to see how it's possible to influence and improve their HRV. If you clip a small sensor to the earlobe, which is connected to the emWave™ monitor, by concentrating you can reduce the coloured lights from red to green, and with practice maintain them on green. Learning what this process feels like internally can help to achieve this independently of the monitor, in time. In the first instance, however, it provides very reassuring feedback that you are able to control your heart coherence and that you can learn to do this at will.

Meditation

Once the preserve of Eastern philosophies and more recently of New Age ideas, meditation is increasingly being recognized as a useful tool with which to overcome and manage some of the worst excesses of twenty-first-century life, not least the damage done by continually working without any downtime. In 1992, the Dalai Llama invited Harvard-trained neuroscientist Richard Davidson from the University of Wisconsin-Madison in the US to visit Dharamsala and see for himself the effects of meditation. Most scientists at the time had no evidence to support the idea that the simple act of thinking could change the way the brain worked. One experiment involved eight Buddhist monks who had meditated for over 10,000 hours and were classed as 'adepts', and ten volunteers who had been trained in meditation for one week at Davidson's laboratory. All those participating in this research, monks and volunteers alike, were asked to meditate on compassion and love. All the monks, and two of the novice volunteers, showed evidence of an increase in gamma brain waves during meditation. What's more, after they stopped meditating, while the levels of gamma brain waves in the volunteers' brains soon returned to normal, this was not the case with the monks. Their brains had been permanently changed through their long experience of meditation. This was the first objective evidence of the way thinking could change brain activity in beneficial ways that could be utilized by anyone who chose to learn this skill. As a result, meditation is becoming more mainstream and is increasingly recommended by health workers and educationalists alike.

'Hundreds of books have been written about the benefits of meditation and many scientific studies have been published', says Vincent Baasch who, in 2008, launched his fifty-minute meditation classes for stressed-out workers in London's business sector. He continues:

Most people coming to meditation for the first time do so in order to manage stress more effectively. Athletes speak of enhanced physical performance. Business people speak of increased concentration and mental performance. Artists speak of improved creativity. Others speak of better energy levels, a stronger immune system and a more positive outlook on life and its challenges. And spiritually minded people may speak of a connection to a bigger or deeper consciousness.

'Anyone who knows how to think can meditate', said Maharishi Mahesh Yogi, the man who brought Transcendental Meditation® (a term that is registered to him) from the East to the West in the late 1950s, and with whom The Beatles famously studied in the 1960s. The film director David Lynch is also a proponent, and, as we have seen in Chapter Seven, his David Lynch Foundation provides training in meditation for children and students. And certainly, while meditation practices lie at the core of many religious and spiritual practices, from Buddhism to yoga, it is a skill that anyone can learn and is increasingly being advocated for physical as well as psychological well-being.

While it's true that meditation will improve concentration abilities, it's also true that in order to learn meditation skills, you need to concentrate. So there is a double benefit, because the practice of meditation is also a way to practise concentration; the two are inextricably linked. However, like concentration, learning to meditate takes both time and application. Although it is entirely possible to be self-taught, there is also a role for a teacher, or guide, especially in the early stages. This need not have any spiritual dimension, but can be an access point from which each of us can build our own practice.

Mindfulness

The concept of mindfulness is central to Buddhist teaching, and is sometimes related to meditation, but it's not restricted to either and its practice is open to anyone wanting to live life in a more focused and aware way. Mindfulness, as a way of living, rather than the application of a spiritual practice, is a process of bringing purposeful attention to bear on any activity under-

⊕ KEY POINTERS FOR MEDITATION

Start with the breathing, which lies at the core of meditation practice and allows an entry point. (See breathing
exercise on page 215.)

○ Get into a routine, where you apply yourself to the
   practice for ten minutes minimum, twice a day,
   and then build on this. Do this in the quiet, without
   interruption.

○ Sit in a comfortable, upright position.

○ Find an external point of focus, often referred to as a
   yantra – some like to focus on a candle flame, a lotus
   flower, or an abstract picture or symbol, like the Hindu
   depiction of the mantra Om – or an internal point of
   focus that you can also visualize in your mind's eye.

○ Use a mantra, a repeated sound that, through its
   vibrations and repetition, resonates and helps increase
   focus and attention to a state of full awareness where
   you are fully present, but your mind and body are
   still. A mantra need not be a spiritual word, but many
   choose to use the Hindu word 'Om' or 'Aum', which
   dates back many thousands of years. Often the mantra
   is extended into the phrase *om namah shivaya*, which
   is literally a salutation to the Hindu god Shiva, but
   can be more broadly interpreted as a salutation to
   the divine spark of life in all of us. Another popular
   Tibetan Buddhist mantra is *om mani padme hum*,
   which translates as 'om, the jewel of the lotus' and
   represents the symbolism of the lotus flower, and how
   its many beautiful petals unfold like the potential of
   our consciousness. Using a mantra with a number of
   syllables, rather than just the extended hum of Om,
   also relates well to the rhythm of breathing.

▶

○ When alone, it's useful to say the mantra out loud quietly, so that the rhythm and vibrations of saying it aid your initial concentration, and then move to saying it silently inside your head.

○ Start with short periods of time – ten minutes – and build on this.

○ Aim to practise every day, twice a day, so that it becomes part of your daily routine.

taken. This activity can be as varied as doing the washing up or performing brain surgery. The point is to be in the moment of the doing, rather than distracted by thoughts, ideas, worries or preoccupations, just allowing for an absorption in what you are doing at that moment.

Mindfulness could be seen as a restrictive process, rigidly focusing on one thing to the exclusion of all else, when in fact it's a liberating process that allows for expansion and creativity, as focusing on 'the doing' of a task frees up, rather than restricts, thoughts. If you focus on something about which you have little or no knowledge, it can be a way of gaining knowledge. Watching a game of football, for example, if you have no initial interest in or understanding of the game, will be baffling at first but, if you stay with it, a sense of purpose and different patterns of play and structure emerge; you begin to engage with what the players are trying to do, you notice their skill and it begins to make some sort of sense. But if you had not stayed with it, uninhibited by your own emotions and preconceived ideas, then you would not have gained this insight. And this can be applied to anything. Mindfulness opens up new ways of being present in the moment, and this searching, active attentiveness can become integrated and, as it were, second nature to you with all the benefits that can bring. Looked at in this way, it becomes obvious how useful this approach can be to improving concentration skills. Just by turning your attention, or mindfulness, into what you are doing automatically improves concentration.

T'ai chi

T'ai chi chuan originated as a Chinese martial art, but in true Eastern philosophy it was not enough to just train the body in this martial art: it was equally important to train the mind. Its original study involved three main principles:

○ Health, through the relief of the physical effects of stress on the body.
○ Meditation, through the focus and calmness of the physical movements, which is a key component of optimal health.
○ Self-defence, which requires an understanding of the philosophy of yielding and responding to an attack, rather than meeting it with an opposing force.

The sequence of movements and poses of t'ai chi, a kind of moving meditation that is designed to balance internal energy, is performed with a clarity and focus that require concentration while also enhancing it. Amazingly, in spite of its slow, low-impact movements, t'ai chi uses as much energy as surfing, and almost as much as downhill skiing! When it comes to health benefits, cardiovascular fitness, flexibility and balance are all improved, while some studies have also shown t'ai chi's effectiveness for improving outcomes following stroke, after surgery, for pain control in chronic ailments like osteoarthritis and for alleviating anxiety and depression. It can even help reduce the severity of diabetes. Hardly surprising, then, that in the US, t'ai chi has become one of the fastest-growing fitness and health-maintenance activities, fast approaching yoga in popularity.

Movements are very precise, but relaxed and controlled, and the breathing has to be coordinated with them, becoming slower and deeper. In order to harmonize and balance the movements of t'ai chi, you need to be very focused and this requires concentration. With regular practice of t'ai chi, the ability to concentrate becomes easier and can then be drawn upon, even without doing specific t'ai chi exercises. Although it would be possible for t'ai chi to be self-taught, in order to learn the correct posture and body movements attending classes with a teacher is more beneficial in the early stages. Once learned, daily practice can be complemented with occasional class attendance to ensure continuing good practice, and also for the social aspect of it. The other beauty of t'ai chi is that it's suitable for all age groups, from childhood to old age. In fact, for the elderly, it can help reduce the incidence of falls, because of the improvement to balance and physical strength.

Alexander Technique

You may not think that your posture would have much to do with your ability to concentrate, but as we saw in Chapter Two poor posture saps energy and that can have an impact on how easy you find it to focus. Your posture may be good enough, but if your day-to-day occupation involves long hours of sitting, it's unlikely that your posture is perfect and not least because we are built for movement, which means being sedentary will always create postural patterns that can be detrimental. Combine this with long hours spent using a computer and, for many of us, the die is cast. Reviewing your posture, and how you use your body when you move, will support your efforts to improve your concentration levels.

The Alexander Technique was devised by Frederick Matthias Alexander, an actor born in Tasmania in 1896, who having experienced voice and breathing problems himself, discovered he could alleviate these by improving his posture. His aim was to unlearn the postural habits that he discovered were impeding the health of his voice and relearn those habits which restored his voice and breath to optimum health. The Alexander Technique doesn't just improve physical coordination (which will have a therapeutic effect) but, because it also demands psychological awareness to improve these patterns of posture and movement, also effects a general self-improvement that affects poise, impulse control and attention.

It's no surprise then that for over twenty years, the Alexander Technique has been included in the training of Israeli Air Force pilots, precisely because it has been found to improve their coordination and reaction times. It's also useful for others who need to use their bodies well while they make repeated and precise physical movements, from dentists to musicians. An efficient and coordinated use of the body improves coordination.

The Society of Teachers of the Alexander Technique (STAT) in the UK have defined the technique and its benefits as helping you to identify and prevent the harmful postural habits that aggravate, or may even be the cause of, stress, pain and under-performance. You will learn how to release tension and rediscover a restored balance of mind and body. With increased awareness you can:

○ be poised without stiffness
○ move gracefully and powerfully with less effort
○ be alert and focused with less strain
○ breathe and speak more easily and freely
○ be calm and confident.

As one STAT pupil put it, 'It allows me to rest my mind, leaves mental space, and therefore helps with decision making and contemplation, plus it improves my energy levels. It's the single best method for achieving all this that I have met in my life.'

> ### ◎ POSTURE EXERCISE
>
> Imagine someone dropping an ice cube down your back
> – or actually try it! – and see what happens to your posture.
> The shock of the cold makes you gasp, which immediately
> draws in your abdominal muscles while straightening and
> drawing your shoulders back and down. This in turn makes
> you drop your chin. Hey presto, your posture is improved!
> Now try to keep it that way.

Sports and exercise activities

We have already seen how beneficial exercise is to the brain.
Not only does it increase the body's oxygen intake, which the
brain needs to function, but it also stimulates neurogenesis,
the creation of new brain cells. But another aspect of exercise
and sporting activity is that, because it makes your body do
specific things that often involve coordination, balance and re-
sponsiveness, you have no choice but to really concentrate on
what you are doing. Also, if you are exercising in a way that
challenges you to the point of your maximum ability, you have
to concentrate. Factor in the element of competitiveness that
exists in many sports and, in fact, often motivate the game,
combined with rules within which you have to operate, and
the clear goals you are aiming for and it's obvious that you
have to concentrate. So, whatever the physical activity that is
demanding your concentration in order for you to succeed, it
can become a useful training ground for other aspects of life in
which your ability to succeed will also be influenced by your
ability to concentrate.

Creating space in your life where you have an opportunity for regular physical activity which exercises your body,
whether this is a regular game of football or squash with your

mates after work, or a Pilates or yoga class, walking around the park or swimming, your mind will benefit just as much as your body. If motivation is an initial problem, remove the element of choice and – in the words of the Nike ad – just do it, because the doing of it will generate feel-good hormones in the brain that are their own reward, and will help motivate you to do it again.

Another important aspect of the active leisure opportunities that regular exercise offers is that it allows you to experience those high-challenge, high-skill moments when your concentration is completely focused on what you are doing. Being 'in the zone', or experiencing 'flow', can be seen on the faces of Wimbledon champions, Tiger Woods or on the face of your own 6-year-old running the egg-and-spoon race on school sports day.

YOGA

Now one of the most popular leisure/exercise activities of the twenty-first century, among both sexes, yoga comes in all sorts of shapes and sizes, which can be tailored to all ages and abilities. What started out as an extension of Eastern philosophy has now become the exercise of choice for many who already benefit from this discipline, which combines flexibility with strength, demands a focus on the breathing and, as a result, will help increase your concentration skills.

PILATES

Again, as in yoga, in Pilates there is an emphasis on breathing, as you do very precise and controlled exercises that aim to balance both sides of the body, while improving 'core stability' – that girdle of internal abdominal muscles that support the back.

SWIMMING

Swimming is another activity that can be done and enjoyed on many different levels. It is also an activity that requires a certain amount of coordination and stamina, combined with correct breathing. In the UK, it's one of the nation's favourite activities, with around 12 million adults now swimming regularly. However, although they do it, many have never been taught to swim correctly, and can miss out on the full benefits because their breathing is haphazard, their confidence in the water is poor and they are unable to swim for any length of time. If you feel that swimming is a way that could help you focus more in everyday life, but you need to learn to do it more productively, find a teacher. In the UK, Alexander Technique teacher Steven Shaw, himself a former competitive swimmer, has devised the Shaw Method of Swimming, which he uses to teach a way of swimming that maximizes the body's movement in water and coordinates breathing correctly. Once these two factors are successfully combined, swimming becomes more efficient and it is easier to concentrate on the process, rather than panting in a haphazard manner through the water.

WALKING

You walk to get from A to B – from the sitting room to the kitchen to get a cup of coffee – and never give it a second thought. Think about it now, because integrating walking into your daily life, whether in an effort to improve your health and fitness levels or just to increase your general mobility, is a good way of counteracting a sedentary lifestyle. Walking a little faster than normal – so that you could still talk, but not sing, for example – immediately increases its health benefits. Regular walking improves muscle tone in your legs, while also raising your heart rate, and so will very quickly contribute to your overall fitness. However, it's the benefits to the brain that are often underestimated: all exercise encourages neurogenesis, and if this is enhanced by engaging with your surroundings as you walk, through the practice of mindfulness (walking in a way that consciously improves your posture and breathing), you can amplify the benefits. Just twenty minutes a day, three times a week, will improve your mood, your blood pressure and your waistline too. What's to lose?

SEX

A good sex life is good for your health – official. You may not see an immediate link between sex and concentration, but good sex, where both partners are fully engaged, intimate and focused on each other to the exclusion of all else, is an act of concentration as well as love. Sex is also good physical exercise, it reduces stress, it triggers the release of positive hormones like oxytocin that create a feeling of well-being and it helps you sleep better. The only proviso really is that it is sex within an enduring, loving relationship, rather than a succession of one-night stands, that makes the difference. So, if you need no other reason to improve your sex life, do so to improve your concentration!

Conclusion

○ **We take it for granted, but our breathing is no small miracle in itself** and by learning how to concentrate on the breath – a technique you can learn in yoga or meditation classes – you will develop your overall powers of concentration. Gentle breathing exercises help you stay more focused, while learning to meditate can help generate more of the feel-good gamma brain waves that will help you stay calm and concentrated, even in a crisis.

○ **Physical exercise can help improve how well you concentrate because it actively promotes neurogenesis** – the brain's ability to make new cells. It also helps keep the mind and body connected and the brain focused and engaged. Whether you walk to work, take a weekly yoga class or play football with the over-40s, keep exercising, because it keeps your brain working and the concentration skills you develop can easily be transferred to other areas of your life.

○ **Simply paying to attention to what you do and how you do it is another great habit to get into.** This is what some people call 'mindfulness' and is an excellent tool for enhancing concentration skills. If you are mindful of what you are saying or doing, you are not being distracted by anything else. You are, truly, present in the moment and in the power of 'you' and your ability to stay focused and to concentrate. There is no better feeling and no better way to harness the benefits of concentrating and reaping all the lifelong benefits that come with that skill.

○ **Good sex (in the context of a loving and intimate relationship) is good for you and can even help with the art of concentration.** When both partners are fully engaged and focused on each other to the exclusion of all else, the act of love becomes an act of concentration too. Sex is also good physical exercise: it helps reduce stress, triggers the release of positive hormones including the well-being hormone oxytocin and will help sleep better so that, the following day, you will be rest and content which will . . . guess what? Help you concentrate better too.

Bibliography

Barlow, Wilfred, MD, *The Alexander Technique: How to Use your Body without Stress*, Healing Arts Press, 1990

Baron, Renée, *What Type Am I? Discover Who you Really Are*, Penguin Books, 1998

Begley, Sharon, *Train Your Mind, Change Your Brain: A Groundbreaking Collaboration between Neuroscience and Buddhism*, Ballantine Books, 2007

Biddulph, Steve, *The Secret of Happy Children*, Thorsons, 1999

Brealey, Erica, *The Spirit of Meditation*, Cassell Illustrated, 2004

Bryan, Mark, Cameron, Julia, and Allen, Catherine, *The Artist's Way at Work*, William Morrow Quill Edition, 1999

Burns, Dr David, *Feeling Good: The New Mood Therapy*, Avon Books, 1999

Csikszentmihalyi, Mihaly, *Finding Flow: The Psychology of Engagement with Everyday Life*, Basic Books, 1997

Fontana, Professor David, *Learn to Meditate*, Duncan Baird Publishers, 1998

— and Slack, Ingrid, *Teaching Meditation to Children*, Watkins Publishing, 2007

Gallagher, Winifred, *Rapt: Attention and the Focused Life*, The Penguin Press, 2009

Gerhardt, Sue, *Why Love Matters: How Affection Shapes a Baby's Brain*, Routledge, 2004

Gibb, Barry J., *The Rough Guide to the Brain*, Rough Guides, 2007

Glouberman, Dr Dina, *The Joy of Burnout*, Skyros Books, 2002

Griffey, Harriet, *The Art of the Nap*, MQ Publications, 2004

Grunfeld, Nina, *The Big Book of Me: Become your Own Life Coach*, Short Books, 2006

Goddard Blythe, Sally, *Attention, Balance and Coordination: The ABC of Learning Success*, Wiley Press, 2009

—, *The Well Balanced Child: Movement and Early Learning*, Hawthorn Press, 2005

—, *What Babies and Children Really Need*, Hawthorn Press, 2008

Harris, Godfrey, and Harris, Kenneth L., *Concentration: How to Focus on the Business at Hand*, The Americas Group, 2001

Honoré, Carl, *In Praise of Slow: How a Worldwide Movement is Challenging the Cult of Speed*, Orion, 2005

Horn, Sam, *Concentration! How to Focus for Success*, Crisp Publications, 1991

—, *ConZentrate: Get Focused and Pay Attention*, St Martin's Griffin, 2001

Jung, Carl, *Psychological Types*, Routledge, 1992

Keirsey, David, and Bates, *Marilyn, Please Understand Me: Character and Temperament Types*, Prometheus Nemesis Book Company, 1984

Kirby, Dr Amanda, *Dyspraxia: Developmental Co-ordination Disorder*, Souvenir Press, 2006

Maas, Dr James, *Power Sleep*, Harper Collins, 1999

Miller, Dr Liz, *Mood Mapping: Plot your Way to Emotional Health and Happiness*, Rodale, 2009

Richardson, Dr Alex, *They Are What You Feed Them*, Thorsons, 2006

Sax, Leonard, MD, PhD, *Boys Adrift: The Five Factors Driving the Growing Epidemic of Unmotivated Boys*, Basic Books, 2007 and 2009

Sax, Leonard, MD, PhD, *Why Gender Matters*, Doubleday, 2005

Servan-Schreiber, Dr David, *Healing Without Freud or Prozac*, Rodale, 2004

Shaw, Steven, and D'Angour, Armand, *The Art of Swimming: A New Direction Using the Alexander Technique*, Ashgrove Publishing, 2001

Singh, Khalsa Dharma, MD, and Stauth, Cameron, *Meditation as Medicine: Activate the Power of your Natural Healing Force*, Simon & Schuster, 2001

—, *The Mind Miracle: The Revolutionary Way to Renew Your Mental Powers*, Arrow Books, 1998

Stafford, Tom, and Webb, Matt, *Mind Hacks: Tips and Tricks for Using Your Brain*, O'Reilly Media Inc., 2004

Useful websites

www.brainshift.co.uk

The Developmental Practitioners' Association website. The DPA is an association of parents and professionals who share a common interest in developmental therapy for children and adults, to help with coordination, developmental and learning difficulties.

www.davidlynchfoundation.org

The Foundation promotes the benefits of Transcendental Meditation® for children and young people, and provides funding for this and research, to assess the effects of the practice on creativity, intelligence, brain functioning, academic performance, ADHD and other learning disorders, anxiety, depression, and substance abuse.

www.fabresearch.org

Food and Behaviour Research (FAB Research) is a charitable organization dedicated both to advancing scientific research into the links between nutrition and human behaviour and to making the findings from such research available to the widest possible audience.

www.heartmath.org

The Institute of HeartMath is an internationally recognized non-profit research and education organization dedicated to heart-based living – people relying on the intelligence of their hearts in concert with their minds to conduct their lives at home, school, work and play.

www.inpp.org.uk

The Institute for Neuro-Physiological Psychology has been pioneering research and treatment into neuro-developmental delay since 1975, using non-invasive, drug-free, remedial programmes.

www.joyofburnout.com

Information about Dr Dina Glouberman, therapist and author of *The Joy of Burnout*, her work, courses and more.

www.lumie.com

Information about the benefits of full-spectrum light therapy, and products.

www.lumosity.com

Website for Lumosity brain training, brain fitness programmes and brain workouts – Reclaim Your Brain™.

www.mentalhealth.org.uk

The Mental Health Foundation is a leading UK charity that provides information, carries out research, campaigns and works to improve services for anyone affected by mental health problems, whatever their age and wherever they live.

www.mindandlife.org

The Mind and Life Institute is dedicated to fostering dialogue and research at the highest possible level between modern science and the great living contemplative traditions, especially Buddhism.

www.nofreudnoprozac.org

Covers the work of Dr David Servan-Schreiber on emotional medicine, and natural approaches to curing stress, anxiety and depression without drugs and without psychotherapy.

www.relax-uk.com

Online resource for the emWave® personal stress reliever products developed by the Institute of HeartMath, and other relaxation aids.

www.schoolfoodtrust.org.uk

The School Food Trust was established by the Department for Education and Skills in September 2005. Its remit is to transform school food and food skills, promote the education and health of children and young people and improve the quality of food in schools.

www.stat.org.uk

Website for the Society of Teachers of the Alexander Technique with information about the technique, learning it, its application and finding a teacher in the UK.

www.tm.org

Website for Maharishi Mahesh Yogi's Transcendental Meditation® programme.

www.lizmiller.co.uk

Website for Dr Liz Miller, author of Mood Mapping, covering her work on mood management and positive mental health.

www.whygendermatters.com

Medical doctor and psychologist Dr Leonard Sax's extensive research on the science of sex differences between girls and boys is explored here, with his thesis on the benefits of single sex education.

www.youthatrisk.org.uk

Youth at Risk is a charity that designs and delivers transformational training and coaching programmes for young people and the professionals that support them.

Index

Page numbers in *italic* refer to boxes and diagrams.